Building Entrepreneurial People

A Step-by-Step Guide to Business Development for Every Member of the Firm

Allan S. Boress

HARCOURT BRACE PROFESSIONAL PUBLISHING

A Division of
Harcourt Brace & Company
SAN DIEGO   NEW YORK   LONDON

HARCOURT BRACE and Quill is a registered trademark of Harcourt Brace & Company.

Printed in the United States of America

ISBN: 0-15-602419-5

To Christine,
my loving and supportive wife,
who allows me to travel the world to conduct my life's work.

Acknowledgments

This book would never have been written without the persistence of John DeRemigis at Harcourt Brace. He managed the process of getting it published and managed me to make sure it was finished. Thank you, John.

As always, I could never complete anything without the invaluable assistance of Stella Ashen, our firm's Director of Marketing and Client Relations.

I would also like to thank Michael Cummings for his contributions on the thought processes and actions of the top business producers, and my son, Jonathan Boress, for his meticulous and excellent proofreading.

Finally, none of this could have been written without my CPA firm's clients, those magnificent people who have allowed me to see how they have been successful these past fifteen years.

Contents

1 Introduction   1

2 CPAs Are Reluctant Entrepreneurs   4

3 Obstacles to Effective Business Development   11

4 Producing Entrepreneurs   15

5 Hiring Entrepreneurs   19

6 Developing Entrepreneurs—Emulating the Right
Role Models   32

7 Developing Entrepreneurs—Guiding Rainmakers   46

8 Developing Entrepreneurs—Encouraging
Entrepreneurial Behavior   54

9 Developing Entrepreneurs—Accountability, Support, and
Management   61

10 Motivating People to Action   75

Action Plan   85

Self-Study CPE Program   89

Index   101

1

Introduction

Most effective rainmakers are born that way or are the result of the environment they grew up in. Many accountants, however, have learned to be entrepreneurs. This Executive Report will assist you and your firm in identifying and creating the type of business-development-oriented partner that is necessary to compete and grow in the 1990s and beyond.

This report represents the collective knowledge I have gained by working with and interviewing hundreds of professional service providers and firms over the past 15 years. There is no theory here; I have discussed only proven ways firms like yours have created entrepreneurial partners. This information is presented in a systematic format you can put to work in your firm immediately.

The importance of business development

New business is the lifeblood of every CPA firm. Some firms today are being forced to merge with other firms, are being bought out under less than desirable circumstances, or are slowly going out of business before the partners' eyes because not enough new clients and new work are coming in. As the founders and rainmakers of numerous firms retire (or hope to), many discover that their fellow partners and staff simply are not interested in—or capable of—developing the business.

Most firms were started and developed by entrepreneurs. These people brought in business because they had to in order to eat and pay the mortgage. Often, these entrepreneurs did such a good job of bringing in work that they had to hire others to help them with the workload. Customarily, those hired were not entrepreneurs by nature—they became accountants because they liked the technical aspects of accounting, not because they wanted to manage and develop a business.

I have observed that the typical CPA firm's way of doing business is exactly the opposite that of a business that wants to grow most successfully. Our profession is endemic—from the schooling we receive to the way we manage our businesses—to creating accountants who grind the work away, not entrepreneurs.

Profound changes in the accounting profession

Jay Nisberg, a consultant based in Ridgefield, Conn., believes the accounting community will endure ongoing troubles over the next few years: increased turnover, fewer would-be partners, more litigation difficulties, more sexual harassment problems, and more difficulty staying state-of-the-art.

According to Nisberg, the 1990s bring a new era of competition for CPAs. "More than ever before, entrepreneurial CPAs are going to succeed in this decade and beyond," he says. He believes that "the traditional reactionary CPA firm way of doing business" will no longer be effective in this more competitive environment.

Nonattest versus attest work

Most CPA firms are already going far beyond the traditional services offered by accounting firms. By expanding into nonattest consulting engagements, these innovative firms find that they are able to realize higher fees and to better serve their clients' needs. Going beyond mere accounting results in happier clients and stronger relationships. Also, promoting business consulting services is a great way to bring in new clients.

Accountants are in a far better position to consult with their clients than their attorneys or bankers. Most lawyers are not trained in business, and some bankers cannot even read a financial statement. Sadly, most CPAs ignore the value and potential profit of consulting and focus on the same kinds of client services accountants offered thirty years ago.

Being a good consultant requires a broader interest base than that of the typical technician. Entrepreneurial CPAs are usually the best suited to business consulting, and so are the most likely to build such a practice.

New challenges

Nisberg cites the following reasons for increased competition in the accounting profession:

- The market for accounting services is shrinking; more companies are themselves doing the kinds of services that CPA firms once provided exclusively.

- A significant number of smaller local practices have been created as spin-offs of numerous larger firms and the shrunken Big Eight.

- More individuals want to work for local rather than national CPA firms because local firms generally allow accountants to exert more control over their lives.

- The trickle-down theory has taken hold; many companies believe they are being better served by local practices than national firms.

- National firms with strong marketing arms are more aggressively soliciting smaller clients.

- Entrepreneurial CPAs are leaving more traditional firms.

- The cost of doing business for CPAs in the 1990s has increased dramatically over that in the 1980s, while partners' salaries have been relatively flat.

- Clients have become more fee-sensitive, and loyalty has virtually disappeared.

The profession has also changed with regard to its product mix. No longer do audits and tax work make up the bulk of the services provided at progressive firms. Far more money can be made and more value provided to clients through nonattest consulting services.

All of these factors indicate that, to succeed in the coming years, accounting firms must be more entrepreneurial. Because accounting practices are equal to no more than the sum of the characteristics and abilities of individuals working within them, those firms that can attract and build entrepreneurs will gain more than their share of success.

2

CPAs Are Reluctant Entrepreneurs

To help your firm build entrepreneurs, consider the following reasons CPAs do not bring in business.

Colleges promote technical competence as the basis for success

Although most colleges today claim to be producing more well-rounded accounting school graduates, I have yet to meet a single person who has taken a course in a School of Accountancy on managing and improving client relationships, managing a CPA firm, or building a practice. This largely one-sided, technically oriented education has prepared accounting graduates for entry-level positions at most CPA firms, but has not prepared them for the real world. It is up to accounting firms to shift new graduates away from total concentration on technical competence.

The profession attracts a certain kind of person

Most CPAs did not choose their profession so they could spend their careers marketing and selling professional services. Only about 10% of the accountants I meet are natural salespeople.

Accounting firms go to great lengths to hire the brightest students, many of whom have spent their nights and weekends studying rather than interacting socially with their peers. This staffing strategy has served accounting firms well until the recent years of profound competition.

No time to sell

By far the most frequent excuse CPAs use for not selling is lack of time. Many accountants are compensated on the basis of billable hours and so focus on doing the work, not bringing it in. When I started out in public accounting, my boss wanted me to be charged out 110% of the time.

Indeed, lack of time in one's daily schedule is a fact of life for most business people, and CPAs are not salespeople. Salespeople are supposed to be spending all of their time selling and serving their clients. CPAs, on the other hand, have work that has to get out. Of course, lack of time gives those not inclined to bring in business the perfect excuse.

However, there are very busy CPAs who do find the time to sell, even during busy season, because they really want to. There is a part of every work day that is a perfect time to sell more business—lunch time.

Lunch is one part of every day that is usually spent alone or with one's co-workers. Even during busy season, accountants usually find time to eat. Your firm's staff members should be investing some of those lunch hours with clients, referral sources, and prospective clients. Consider having them spend four to twelve lunches a month selling more business.

CPAs should realize they are selling all the time—such as when they are persuading the client to take a certain action, getting people in the office to do work for them, or keeping their eyes and ears open for service opportunities with existing and prospective clients.

Firms do not require personal marketing skills for advancement

Even in today's competitive environment, there are still some firms that promote to partner staff members who have not demonstrated an ability to bring in business. These firms often wind up with staff accountants who dictate the firm's policies and earn partnership salaries without bearing the burden of contributing new business to the firm.

Consider your firm: Are its staff members abundantly aware that to attain partnership they will have to prove that they can bring in business? Do not wait for them to become motivated to sell after they make partner. By then, it will be too late.

Firms do not allow risk

CPAs are probably the most risk-averse people in the world. Although avoiding risks is correct when handling audits and certain other client matters, this attitude usually permeates other areas of the firm. However, if you examine your successful clients' businesses, taking risks is often a major part of their success.

Not only calculated risks should be promoted in CPA firms. Many of my clients have become hugely successful by "taking a flyer" on an idea. If you limit your firm to taking only calculated risks, the advantage or idea could pass or become stale by the time you have analyzed the situation.

Consider the automobile business. One of the most revolutionary ideas in that industry in the past thirty years was the product of one man's willingness to follow his instincts and take huge risks that could have destroyed both his career and his company.

Lee Iacocca took the risk of bringing out a vehicle that did not fit into the existing categories. While attempting to save Chrysler from bankruptcy, he debuted the minivan, creating a new class of vehicle, neither car nor truck. One reason he left Ford was that company's refusal to make such a vehicle.

On the basis of one idea, Iacocca turned Chrysler into a phenomenally prosperous company and created a totally new market segment. Not only did Iacocca risk his career and Chrysler's financial well-being, but he also risked the company's reputation.

Similarly, Bill Gates said in a recent interview he and Microsoft risked the entire company on the success or failure of Windows. Remember that Microsoft was already phenomenally successful because of the MS-DOS operating system for IBM-PC compatible computers.

If Chrysler or Microsoft had been run by CPAs, neither of these revolutionary products would have been produced. If people are afraid to take risks in areas beyond their accounting and tax duties, they will never be entrepreneurs.

CPAs dislike selling

Approximately 90% of CPAs dislike selling. This attitude is probably one reason they became CPAs in the first place. If they loved selling, chances are they would have pursued a career in sales.

Luckily, it is not necessary to like something to do it. Not much would be accomplished if we waited to like a task before we attempted it.

CPAs do not know how to sell

Human beings in general, and CPAs in particular, tend to embark only upon those pursuits they feel confident about. Every day CPAs are told they must bring in business without being given the slightest clue about how to do so effectively. Although each person should be responsible for his or her own career advancement, most accountants rightly believe that if the firm wants them to sell, they should be trained—at the firm's expense—to do so. However, very few firms offer effective training in the ability to persuade others to do what we want them to do.

There is no antidote for the pain of failure

If CPAs fail, they lose clients, lose their licenses, or get sued. The no-failure message usually permeates every level and every function of CPA firms, including business development. Most CPAs will not try to develop their practices if is likely that they will be condemned for failure.

Accounting is a unique profession—anything positive is viewed with suspicion, while negatives are embraced (the principle of conservatism permeates most CPA firms at every level). Statement on Auditing Standards (SAS) No. 54 (Illegal Acts By Clients) says that accountants must exhibit "professional skepticism." CPAs usually follow this tenet when managing their employees, as well as their technical practices.

When selling professional services, one must first fail to succeed. The more you fail, the more business you will sell in the long run. Therefore, failure in bringing in business must be allowed—and even actively promoted—to give CPAs the freedom to succeed at selling.

CPAs assume clients will ask for new services

Many CPAs are reluctant to approach their clients about services they believe the client needs for fear of damaging the relationship. This fear is not without basis; people generally do not like being "sold."

However, clients not approached for additional work can be lost to the sales efforts of other professionals—who then get the kind of high profit work you could do just as well. For example, your client might consult with an outsider when choosing a computer system, but you undoubtedly know the client's records and systems better. The same is true of estate services, tax planning, and many other services your client might need but not know your firm can provide.

By not being forthcoming with clients, CPAs open the door to the sales efforts of other professionals who can, and often do, introduce their competitors to their clients. CPAs often miss the opportunity for the easy sale—easy because the client has already made the decision to do business with the firm. These easy sales can boost the seller's confidence and willingness to take risks.

Also, without proactive CPAs, clients' businesses may not be as healthy and successful as they could be. Most clients would be less concerned about fees if they also made more money and perceived additional value beyond the basic accounting, audit, and tax services most CPA firms provide.

Firms have no action plan

Accountants like to create and work from lists. Without a plan of action or list of activities to follow, they generally stall and accomplish little. Imagine trying to complete an audit without an audit plan. A personal marketing plan is equally important to any business development effort.

To build entrepreneurs, have your firm's staff members set goals for the number of face-to-face contacts they will have every week with clients, prospective clients, and referral sources. Start with one or two a week. At the end of a year, each will have had fifty or more sales opportunities they otherwise would not have had.

Firms have no system of accountability

Unless they are accountable to some person with authority, most CPAs will tend to neglect distasteful tasks like business development. Those firms that have a high participation rate of partners and staff in the business development effort are either blessed with a collection of people who are good at selling or they actively hold each other accountable for bringing in work.

Firms offer no support or recognition

Most CPAs are not motivated to change their behavior by money, unless it represents a substantial part of their total compensation packages. Unless they are already so inclined, 10% or 20% of the collected fees is not going to change someone's behavior.

Many CPA firms have tried, and usually failed, to motivate through monetary bonuses or awards. Fortunately, public accounting generally affords practitioners a comfortable livelihood. One effective way to motivate staff members is to do so psychologically: Make business developers the firm's heroes. Shower them with attention and admiration. Publicize their efforts generously.

Unfortunately, most firms do not recognize sales and marketing successes, and then do not understand why people stop bringing in business. In most firms, negative reinforcement is offered for most behaviors, except perhaps for charging a large number billable hours or bringing in projects below budget. In fact, CPA firms tend to give far too little reinforcement, except when mistakes are made—and then negative reinforcement is used.

Firms have no firm-wide goals

If a firm does not have a set goal for growth or new business, any expansion will be accidental. People like to participate in team efforts where everyone is on the same wavelength. They need to know what is expected and wanted of them.

Without a firm-wide strategic plan and a methodology for implementing it, people tend to go off in their own directions, duplicating efforts or making no effort at all. Everyone in the firm needs to know exactly what the firm's goals are. Also, a comparison of actual versus planned results should be shared with the entire staff so they can see any progress being made. When staff members know what the firm's goals are, they can operate on the same wavelength. Having everyone move toward a common objective creates a group dynamic that breeds creativity, action, and entrepreneurial behavior.

Most firms, however, have no plan. Some partner groups hide their goals from their employees, eliminating this powerful method of building a practice.

CPAs expect clients to be permanent

When I first started out in public accounting, clients were referred to as "annuities." In some firms, they still are.

Unfortunately, client retention can no longer be taken for granted. Taking clients for granted because you are a good CPA and have had the clients for several years causes the firm to neglect its clients. If your firm does not recognize that its clients need to be won over every day, the clients will take their business elsewhere when they perceive it is in their best interest.

Firms must continuously impress upon their staff members that they must constantly look for new ways to serve their clients. Usually the best way to make that happen is through selling.

Firms' leaders do not sell

Sometimes, firms seek to hire me to work only with their staff members to help them bring in more business. The partners are not interested in this sort of training—it is beneath them.

That approach does not work. Partners must lead the way. CPAs will follow the partnership's lead to bring in business. If the partners do it and it is well publicized and clearly expected, others will as well. Even if a partner is not particularly gifted at business development, the idea that everyone is involved in the effort will motivate staff members to behave as entrepreneurs.

3

Obstacles to Effective Business Development

The previous chapter discussed what prevents individuals from becoming entrepreneurs, and actively marketing and selling. This chapter will review what prevents firms from achieving marketing and business development success, complicating and harming the efforts of individuals who want to build their practices.

Many accounting firms are penny wise and dollar foolish

In most CPA firms, everything tends to be viewed as a cost rather than an investment. The partners bleed the business dry by withdrawing salaries and profits, leaving little to be reinvested in the business for new technology, training, facilities, or other improvements.

CPA firms most often neglect to set aside the time or money to train their staff members in the "soft" areas of personal marketing, selling, and client relationship management. Also, most CPAs fail to provide the monetary incentives that will motivate those people in their firms who already have the entrepreneurial skills.

Accountants operate with blinders on

The attitude in most firms is: "If it ain't broke, don't fix it." As long as business is good today, it will always be so. CPA firms operate more like "job shops" than like businesses. In a job shop, everyone keeps his or her nose to the proverbial grindstone and hopes that business will continue to come in as it always has. This nose-to-the-grindstone mentality prevents many CPAs from accomplishing most of the important activities crucial to creating a successful business: planning, organizing, directing, communicating, and coordinating.

Accountants want to do it themselves

Some firms create their own marketing plans and training. However, CPAs are trained in financial statement preparation and taxation—and often little else. Most accountants are simply not knowledgeable enough about marketing to create effective business development programs.

CPAs generally see marketing as some grand scheme that requires careful plotting and planning. Many firms formulate a master plan, which winds up sitting on a shelf gathering dust. Direction, creativity, motivation, and impetus often must come from an expert in the field of marketing who has a different idea of the marketplace and what it takes to succeed in it.

Too often, in-house marketing and training programs, designed to save money, cause many firms to fail to provide the information and support needed to produce rainmakers.

CPA firms' compensation systems are wrong

CPAs love to discuss compensation plans for partners because they mistakenly believe therein lies the secret to producing rainmakers. In fact, the people who bring in business will continue to do so because they see new business for what it truly is: the lifeblood of the firm. However, rainmakers need to have the proper monetary incentives to encourage them to produce to their capabilities and to develop their skills.

Often rainmakers earn less than their partners because their firm's system of compensation is designed to reward billable hours. In other firms, the "pot" is split evenly after partners' salaries are deducted from net profits at the end of the year. This penalizes those who bring in business and rewards the technicians, who often do nothing to build the practice.

Some partners discourage staff members' business development efforts

Partners often respond surprisingly to newer staff members' sales successes. Some may feel that effective marketing by junior accountants threatens their own images or reputations. Others may take credit for the staff members' work. Still others may try to discourage difficult or unprofitable new business, and may thereby discourage aspiring partners' sales efforts altogether.

Be careful not to stifle budding entrepreneurs' interest in business development. Instead, be grateful that your staff members are expending the time and effort necessary to build your practice. With nurturing, guidance, and positive reinforcement, future rainmakers will hone their skills at identifying and securing the kind of work your firm really wants.

Accountants want a quick fix

The process of bringing in business requires education, experience, and a change in behavior that cannot occur in one day. As with any situation where new habits and change in behavior are required, it takes time and continued, monitored learning. Learning how to market, sell, and manage client relationships does not happen in a day, just as people who have a problem with alcohol or drugs cannot change their lives in a day. Both situations require an investment of time, effort, and energy.

CPA firms lack an entrepreneur-friendly environment

Some accountants foolishly spend money looking for anything that will allow them to avoid direct involvement in marketing—like glossy brochures, advertising, and expensive public relations campaigns. Firms can waste tens of thousands of dollars with public relations firms and advertising agencies, only to get little or no return on their investments. The only factor that can always be counted on to build a practice is personal marketing.

Firms are afraid to train their staff members

Many CPAs want to keep their staff members handicapped in terms of business development. They fear that improving the skills, interests, knowledge, and confidence of their employees will empower these employees to leave the firm, taking clients and building their own practices.

Firms have no control process for business development

For any process to operate successfully, there must be a control function. CPAs are control freaks—most seek control in every aspect of their lives. But less than 2% of CPA firms I encounter attempt to monitor and control their business development processes. Apparently, most CPAs are too busy billing themselves out to manage their businesses.

CPA firms lack leadership

The partnership approach to doing business often lends itself to indecision. To do business effectively in a democratic or collegial environment, there must be strong leadership. Unfortunately, most CPAs are not effective leaders. And without strong, visionary leadership, firms stagnate and eventually die, becoming sitting ducks for more assertive competitors.

CPAs tend to gauge success by looking only at the bottom line, and often manage themselves right out of business. Most successful business people judge success by increased market share, revenues, and customer and client satisfaction.

Many CPA firms are not run like traditional businesses because they do not facilitate leadership. In most firms, the partners and managers are occupied by time-consuming administrative duties that could be accomplished by support or administrative staff members. Also, CPAs tend to be afraid to let anyone else take responsibility for the operation of the firm.

In this chapter, we have discussed what may be holding your firm back from empowering the marketing efforts of individuals and from marketing and business development success. The next chapter will discuss ways to produce entrepreneurs.

4

Producing Entrepreneurs

Like all skills, rainmaking must be learned. There are four distinct ways to develop entrepreneurs within your firm:

- Acquiring
- Mentoring
- Hiring
- Encouraging

Acquiring entrepreneurs

One way to build entrepreneurs that is often overlooked is infecting the firm's culture with a successful entrepreneur who actively brings in business. When acquiring practices, look for those still actively promoted by entrepreneurs. Bringing proactive partners into your firm will not only build your practice but can also set a new mood for the office, adding an urgency for new business.

One firm has successfully developed its practice by systematically searching for and incorporating these kinds of individuals into the firm. The two founding partners have taken it upon themselves to network extensively in the local chapters of their state society, searching for entrepreneurial sole practitioners. By building relationships with these people, they are able to determine whether these people would fit into their firm. If the fit seems good, they make the sole practitioners an offer to join their firm.

Mentoring entrepreneurs

Business producers have traditionally "grown up" in CPA firms through the guidance of more experienced, more entrepreneurial accountants. Those of us fortunate enough to watch, learn from, and be nurtured by such CPAs are pushed into action and told what we do well and what we need to improve.

The success of this technique for developing entrepreneurs is limited to the number of people in your firm who are successful at generating business and who will then take someone under their wing. To be effective mentors, these people must have the ability to teach others what they know.

Unfortunately, most rainmakers are busier than people who do not bring in business. Rainmakers must literally carve out the time to help build future stars.

Dan Fensin, managing partner of Blackman Kallick Bartelstein, Chicago, says his firm uses mentors to develop its future entrepreneurs. "We have a person in our marketing department who works with the managers and supervisors to help them develop their networks," says Fensin. "We also have a program where the partners meet with the staff people regularly. Every person on the staff is assigned to a partner. We call it the `One-On-One' program. We go out with them and have our lunches with them. We talk to them about our own sales and marketing experiences. I've told my staff that there's nothing more exciting than that prospect calling you up saying that you have the work. It's the greatest feeling in the world."

Developing a mentoring program

There are three types of mentoring programs your firm can initiate to encourage entrepreneurial behavior and promote active personal marketing: partner-to-partner mentoring, partner-to-staff mentoring, and staff-to-staff mentoring.

Partner-to-partner mentoring   Working directly with another partner is a sure way for a partner to improve his or her marketing productivity. This process consists of the following steps:

- **Monthly meetings**   Partner "buddies" meet to lay out their marketing goals for the following month. Each partner commits to specific marketing activities during the month, explaining what they are doing and the intended results. The partners question and coach each other about the value and effectiveness of their proposed marketing actions and hold each other accountable for the quantity and quality of the activities. Also, each helps the other avoid letting excuses get in the way of marketing.

  Because the partners discuss their proposed marketing activities, they have an opportunity to see holes and mistakes in each other's plans that otherwise might not be noticed. Additional ideas that are more creative and productive can be generated that might not be thought of individually.

These sessions should take place every month, even during busy season. Personal marketing and selling must not stop even during the busiest time of the year.

- **Accountability** Partners hold each other accountable for the marketing and sales goals of the previous month. Without accountability, goals can be neglected.

- **Brainstorming** Partners discuss ideas for closing deals still in process. Two heads are better than one when it comes to closing strategies.

Partner-to-staff mentoring In addition to the three basic elements of mentoring&goals, accountability, and closing strategies&partner/ staff member meetings should include the following discussions about the partner's career:

- **Personal history** The partner should describe how he or she became involved in the selling and marketing process from the beginning of his or her career.

- **Struggles and failures** Nobody closes every sale. The partner should describe his or her personal struggles in securing business, illustrating that business development cannot be taken for granted or sidelined as unimportant. Often, the only way to learn is by failing. By sharing their sales and marketing mishaps, partners can help staff members avoid similar mistakes. Also, this kind of openness will improve the partner-staff relationship, enabling the staff member to view the partner more realistically, avoiding the usual image of infallibility promoted in so many firms.

- **Successes** Everyone loves a success story. By explaining to the staff member how business was sold or how a certain referral relationship was established, the partner can infuse that person with the excitement he or she experienced. This sort of emotion is contagious; the staff member believes that such successes are attainable, the partner renews his or her enthusiasm about marketing, and both become more productive.

- **Growth** As the partner grows and learns more about the great skills of personal marketing and selling, the staff member can learn and change as well.

- **Encouragement** Helping staff members improve their selling and personal marketing skills demonstrates the support of the partner and of the firm. Positive reinforcement and input is guaranteed to produce far better results than the usual negativity and lack of communication that permeate most CPA firms.

Staff-to-staff mentoring   Staff members with the appropriate levels of experience can serve as mentors to each other in the manner described above.

This chapter identifies four ways to build entrepreneurs and discusses two of those ways: buying and mentoring entrepreneurs. The next chapter will look at hiring the right people in the first place.

5

Hiring Entrepreneurs

To improve your firm's hiring process, start looking at it like a football team looks at the draft process. Usually, football teams expect their high draft choices to begin producing immediately, while other newcomers are introduced into the system incrementally.

"It all starts in the recruiting phase with the kind of person that you hire," says Steven Messing, partner-in-charge of the tax practice at KPMG Peat Marwick, Miami. Marketing problems can be avoided if you hire the right people. Once they are on your firm's payroll and you have invested thousands of dollars in training them, it becomes much more difficult to let them go. Remember Boress' Rule of Employment: "The longer someone works for you arithmetically, the harder they are to fire geometrically."

Be direct with prospective employees

Let interviewees know from the start that your firm is not just hiring more staff accountants. Explain that every employee is responsible for building the firm's business. To be considered for partnership some day, staff members must prove their value by building a powerful referral network and bringing in a material amount of work.

You will lose some candidates you thought you wanted by being this candid. The ones you forfeit would never have brought much business to the firm. Instead, they probably would have impeded the firm's business development effort.

Certain aggressive candidates, the natural rainmakers, will be enticed by your firm's approach to managing its accounting practice and attracted to your emphasis on growth and opportunity. Also, this strategy will help you avoid disappointments later and serve to separate you from every other recruiter on campus.

Hiring right in the first place

People must possess certain abilities to successfully bring in business. Some of these can be taught through a lengthy training process that most CPA firms are not willing to invest in. Other such traits can be identified during the hiring process. By selecting candidates who have these winning attributes, you can guarantee a higher percentage of rainmakers developing within your firm.

CPAs' selling advantages

CPAs already possess certain winning traits that only the best salespeople have. Even candidates coming right out of school possess many of these strengths, which are not often identified as being winning sales characteristics. The existing attributes CPAs and CPA candidates possess include:

- **Intelligence** CPAs tend to be fairly—or even highly—intelligent. Also, they often have the capability to think quickly. These native abilities are important to successful marketing and selling.

- **Dedication** The accounting profession generally attracts only those who understand the value of hard work, diligence, and stamina. They know that public accounting is not an easy ride, especially compared to working in private industry. Those who are attracted to its challenges tend to possess these important attributes, which are vital to sales and personal marketing success.

- **Interviewing skills** It seems that most accountants spend much of their time asking questions of clients, vendors, and referral sources. This familiarity with interviewing, limited though it may be, gives accountants an advantage over typical sales people, who tend to ask too few questions. This is great experience to have as it relates to rainmaking: The best salespeople and marketers ask a lot of questions.

- **Nonthreatening personalities** This tremendous advantage to accountants can facilitate creating a huge book of business. If someone is not threatened by an individual, and that person really listens after asking questions, people will tell the seller just how to sell them.

  Conversely, many salespeople tend to intimidate their customers by making them feel that they are being "sold." When people are scared, they put up their defenses and become much less receptive. CPAs, because they are generally nonthreatening, often overcome this tremendous difficulty.

- **Systematic and methodical organizational skills** Only the very best salespeople have these powerful traits. Yet CPAs either possess them upon entering public accounting or develop them throughout their careers because of the nature of the profession.

  If a person is systematic, organized, and methodical about the way he or she pursues marketing and selling, that person will close much more than his or her share of business. This diligent individual will not allow the opportunities for new business to fall through the proverbial cracks. Unfortunately, most CPA firms do not cultivate an environment that leads to proactive personal marketing and selling, wasting these innate skills.

- **Persistence** Most CPAs had to be pretty darned persistent to pass the exam. For many, passing the exam required determination and application. These traits are wonderful when they are applied to selling and personal marketing.

- **Consistency** Only the top business producers in all of the professions are consistent in their personal marketing and selling. Consistency is a basic requirement of the accounting profession. It is consistency in marketing and selling that separates the winners from the losers in bringing in business. This trait is either innate or developed while working in the profession.

- **Analytical and diagnostic skills** Accountants are taught to figure things out, never taking things for granted or at face value. The skills necessary to do this are marvelous for identifying and looking beneath the surface of selling and marketing opportunities.

- **Documentation skills** The nature of public accounting requires the creation of evidence and documentation. Only the best salespeople follow such a system. Because not all sales are closed on the first interview, building relationships is an ongoing process, not a single event.

  The ability to bring in business is enhanced by creating evidence. This serves as a constant reminder to the seller of his or her position in the sales cycle and of the important attributes that are necessary to maintain and improve client and referral relationships. Without a paper trail, the seller does not know where he or she has been in the selling process, where he or she is now, or where he or she needs to go.

Other requirements for sales success

To ensure the future success of your firm, the following traits should be identified in potential employees. Weed out those who lack them during the hiring process. Many of these characteristics are innate, and no amount of training, attention, or compensation will teach them.

- **Ability to build relationships** The skills necessary to build a book of business and lead a CPA firm are based on one idea: Business is relationships. The days of having business brought to your firm because it is technically proficient have long since passed in most service lines and most areas of the country. To bring in business, CPAs must build relationships with other human beings that are close, friendly, and often intense.

  Those attracted to public accounting tend to be of a certain nature. No matter how much effort goes into denying it, most people attracted to the accounting profession do not perceive themselves as having strengths in building personal relationships. Most effective relationship-builders pursue careers in public relations, advertising, or sales—careers in which one is surrounded by people all day long.

  Certainly, there are accountants who are better at building personal relationships than others. Your firm must identify and hire these people, instead of those who are shy and afraid of interpersonal relationships.

- **Communication skills** Communication skills include the capacity to listen to what people are really saying and the ability to make effective presentations. If people cannot communicate their ideas lucidly, concisely, and enthusiastically—without rambling—they will never be effective sellers or marketers. Sadly, those who are worst at verbal, visual, or written communication tend to want help the least. Avoid future problems by not hiring people who are not already excellent communicators.

- **Willingness to take risks** Accounting may seem to be a fairly safe career, especially considering the basic message accounting students receive: "If you are a competent accountant, you will go far." This sounds simple enough: Work hard, work long, learn all the important aspects of being a great technician, and you will succeed. I have never discovered a single course in any school of accountancy on what it really takes to be successful as a CPA:

managing an accounting practice, marketing and selling accounting and consulting services, managing client relationships, and
getting along and working with people.

Willingness to take risks is another of the greatest attributes of
future rainmakers and entrepreneurs. Often the greatest successes
come from taking the exceptional risk.

Many successes in the accounting profession can be traced to
risks taken by accounting firms and individuals. Eliminate people
who have not shown an ability or desire for risk-taking during
the interview process.

- **Ability to relate to others** The ability to relate to clients and
prospective clients is vital to building a practice. Sadly, most CPAs
cannot understand anything beyond the technical intricacies and
details of accounting and taxes. This inability to relate to the challenges facing clients poisons existing client relationships and prevents new ones.

  Building a practice and dealing with other people depends on
one's ability to connect with other human beings. Accounting,
however, tends to attract those who lack or shy away from this
trait. Pay attention to how interviewees relate to you and others
during the interviewing process. Remember, technicians will best
relate to other technicians. To hire people who will bring in business and get others to help them build the firm's practice, have
more "normal" people than technicians interview prospective
employees.

- **Ability to succeed beyond scholastics** Everyone has to succeed
scholastically to survive the accounting-school selection process
and to pass the CPA exam. However, people who succeed in areas beyond their immediate academic strengths demonstrate the
traits of a winning business developer. The questions asked during the interviewing process will help you discover this.

- **Ability to survive rejection** Personal rejection is part of building a practice. After all, accountants are primarily selling themselves. People who can continue to sell and market despite having their feelings hurt are the true winners in the game of business development.

- **Desire to make a difference** The top business producers in all
the professions are often motivated by things other than wealth.
Material satisfaction is part of the accounting profession. Most
CPAs live quite comfortably. This is one obstacle to motivating

partners and staff members to change their behavior and bring in business solely through compensation.

Accounting's top business producers generally have an intense desire to make a difference in the lives and businesses of their clients, referral sources, and employees. It is this intense desire to help other people that leads to successful business development. Often one has to overcome personal fears to help someone else, such as mentioning a potential area of improvement in a client's business or requesting a referral. The desire to make a difference motivates many entrepreneurs and enables them to move beyond their fears.

You must discover interviewees' real reasons for selecting a career in public accounting. If a prospective employee wants only to make a good living, he or she may be the wrong candidate.

- **Time management skills** The accounting profession is by nature full of unreasonable demands on CPAs' time. Time is an accountant's scarcest asset, yet few CPAs have ever taken a time management course. CPAs must somehow squeeze business development into their daily lives.

  Future entrepreneurs will already have demonstrated an ability to manage their time. Students who have spent their academic careers studying have not faced the same challenges as those who have also found time for a full- or part-time work schedule or a significant campus leadership role. Those who only study are going to expect that their lives as CPAs will encompass their daily work and little more. Weed these people out during the interview process—they are the ones who will constantly complain and make excuses about their involvement in business development.

- **Creativity, curiosity, and lack of complacency** Business developers must be creative in the way they pursue targeted clients or referral sources. To get to the forefront in the business development effort, one must commit to a constant process of learning, so future rainmakers must be curious by nature. Also, budding entrepreneurs should not be too easily satisfied. If people have low expectations of their lives, chances are they will not stretch enough to go beyond their fears and weaknesses.

- **Ability to work through others** It is impossible to build an accounting practice alone. CPAs will always need to have their clients bring them referrals, to motivate referral sources to pass on more business, and to have their employees go the extra mile in client service and other areas to support the business development process. If a CPA cannot accomplish work through the abilities of others, he or she will not be able to lead others or build a successful practice.

- **Persuasive abilities**   Interviewers should determine the amount of interest candidates have in sales and marketing and how they believe it affects one's abilities to succeed as a CPA. Also, discover whether candidates have sales experience and how they feel about selling.

- **Desire and ability to lead**   Entrepreneurs are leaders by definition; sheep do not bring in business. The accounting profession is bereft of natural leaders and is full of people who follow. Unfortunately, followers often become partners and accomplish little because they neither make decisions nor do they have the willingness to take risks.

- **Ability to make decisions quickly**   Only good decision-makers can help others make decisions. If one hesitates to make decisions, he or she will forever be missing sales opportunities.

- **Common sense**   Sales trainer and motivator Al Desarro of Hollywood, Fla., says you cannot teach common sense. I agree.

    Unfortunately, most CPAs lack common sense. For example, in many firms, the people who bring in business often make less than the technicians. Also, some firms spend every available dollar on partners' compensation, failing to invest in their own business in the form of the latest technology, employee training, or contact with clients. In fact, less than 25% of all CPA firms bother to thank their clients on a regular basis, via hand-written holiday cards or gifts. Fewer CPA firms take annual client surveys.

    Consider your most successful clients—do they work in the plant on the machinery knocking out whatsits, or do they invest their time with their customers, referral relationships, suppliers, and managing their business? Most business owners do not spend their time doing detail work that could be delegated to others. Using their common sense, successful business people invest their valuable time and energy in their businesses.

- **Flexibility**   CPAs tend to be quite rigid in their beliefs. The accounting profession is generally black and white, based on rules and regulations, and quite bureaucratic by nature. However, the top business producers have the ability to deal with various kinds of people. Look for this quality during the interview process.

- **Self-motivation**　The single most important trait of budding entrepreneurs is the internal motivation to surpass barriers and succeed despite overwhelming odds—the intense appetite to achieve. Successful rainmakers have demonstrated that they have a strong desire to respond to a challenge, especially in an area where they are not already successful. For example, responding to academic challenges is absolutely necessary in the study of accounting. Future entrepreneurs love challenge and achievement. Look for this drive during the interview process.

Finding people with these attributes is a difficult task, but your firm can avoid future marketing and client relationship problems by hiring the right people in the first place. Of course, there is no perfect candidate. However, most CPA firms do not consider these issues when hiring and then have difficulty motivating their staff to bring in business.

Be more careful when screening candidates, and let them know that your firm is highly selective. The kind of candidate your firm needs to hire is attracted to the challenge of a selective firm.

Qualities to look for in prospective employees

If your firm wants entrepreneurial partners and managers, stop hiring nerds! Hire people that are immediately likable. You cannot change someone's inherent personality without a great deal of time and effort. If an individual has invested most of their life being introverted and shy, do not expect them to change. Stop looking only for good technicians and start seeking people with personalities. Remember that intelligent people can be trained to be good technicians, but personality cannot be taught.

Ask yourself some questions about the candidates: Do you like them immediately? Or do you have to look hard to find something about them you admire? If you are interviewing someone and trying desperately to find something about them that you like, chances are good that the candidate does not have a well-rounded personality or social experience, and your clients and prospective clients will notice this, too.

Technicians tend to hire other technicians, and are often suspicious and critical of people who are outgoing and immediately likeable. J. Paul Getty, one of the world's most successful business people, discusses the subject in his best-selling book *How To Be Rich:*

"Technical knowledge? I'll admit that in this day of complex industrial and business technology, every executive needs a greater degree of technical knowledge. I can sum up my views on the subject by saying that I'd rather try to make a good technician out of a good executive who has no technical knowledge than try to make a good executive out of a good technician who has no executive ability."

By using this approach your firm may hire people who do not become superb technicians, but the greater risk lies in hiring nerds. With a heavily technical staff, there will be no one around to nurture the growth of your practice, build better relationships with your clients, and take over the leadership of the firm.

Concentrate on candidates' outside activities

Look seriously at positions of leadership prospective employees have held on campus or in their current lives. Search for people who are going to make something happen, not wait around to be told what to do.

Ask candidates the following questions:

- What did you do while you were in school?

- What kind of activities have you participated in?

- Were you involved in activities in which you had to deal with people?

- Do you have sales experience?

At Blackman Kallick Bartelstein in Chicago, "We don't hire people who are good with a pencil and can't open their mouth," says Dan Fensin, managing partner. "We look for people-related experience in students; the person who worked in a bank versus the person who did construction. If they have the ability to communicate, there's no reason they can't market or sell accounting services."

"When we hire tax people out of school we look for the best raw talent—and that means not only brain power but also social and communication skills," says Steve Messing of KPMG Peat Marwick, Miami. "We're looking for people who on an overall basis have a very broad perspective on things. We look for people who can certainly render quality tax advice, but at the same time have people skills. Every person we hire, we hire with the intention that someday they will become a partner. . . . We try to envision what that person would be like over the period of time it will take to gain experience to become a partner."

Interview the "real" candidate

Remove candidates from the formal interviewing process to see how they interact with others and what they are really like as human beings. Everyone is on his or her best behavior in a formal setting. CPA firms often hire people they later discover are significantly different from the person they thought they interviewed. Many firms have had extraordinary success in hiring future rainmakers by getting prospective employees into casual clothes and a casual social setting. Taking prospective employees out of the formalized hiring process allows you to meet and observe the "real" person in action.

Some firms make a point of putting prospective employees in social situations, such as a room full of strangers. Others take the candidate and their spouse or significant other to dinner.

Ask the following questions of every interviewer in your firm:

- Is the prospective employee gregarious and friendly? Does he or she appear shy?
- How does the candidate treat his or her spouse? How about the restaurant staff?
- Does the candidate appear hesitant to introduce him- or herself to others? Does he or she stand alone in a group?
- Can the candidate maintain a conversation? Does he or she attempt to engage others in conversation?

Have effective business producers conduct key interviews

It takes an entrepreneur to know one. Technicians often screen out future rainmakers. By involving your firm's entrepreneurs in the interview process, you will quickly identify future rainmakers.

Invest time in the interviewing process

All too often, firms are in a rush to hire a staff accountant. By investing more time in the interviewing process, you decrease the likelihood of hiring the wrong person. Also, interviewing candidates more than once or twice enables you to get to know the person better.

Ask the right questions

Firms often fail to ask questions that will uncover future rainmakers during the hiring process. Remember, the most honest answers to your questions usually emerge outside the traditional interviewing environment. Following is a list of questions accumulated over the years from firms that make a point of hiring the right people:

- *Why have you chosen a career in accounting?* Discover whether the candidate's goal is to hide behind workpapers or computers, or if he or she is interested in the well-rounded experience a career in public accounting can offer. Some people will come right out and say they do not have an interest in dealing with people or are looking for a career that will insulate them from personal interactions.

- *What are your ultimate career goals?* If candidates are removed from the formalized process, they will tell you much more than you might expect. For example, one prospective employee said she planned to spend no more than three years in public accounting before moving on to a career in private industry. Another candidate casually mentioned that his brother was a CPA who had left his firm to start his own practice, taking a lot of clients with him. The candidate thought this was a great idea!
  Still another prospective employee told an interviewer that her ultimate career goal was to be managing partner of a CPA firm. This person later climbed to the partnership faster than any previous employee, and is now in line to become the next managing partner.

- *What is your idea of fun?* Does the candidate enjoy reading books, watching movies, or being involved in people-related activities?

- *How would you really feel about being responsible for bringing in business?* Discuss this topic candidly before your firm invests thousands of dollars in training a reluctant business producer.

- *How would you feel about investing in your own personal skills to get ahead?* Entrepreneurs must be willing to go the extra mile to meet their career goals.

- *How would you feel about meeting clients and referral sources on your own time?* Set the future employee's expectations now.

- *If you did not go into public accounting, what would you like to do?* This will give you an idea of the candidate's ultimate career goals and work-related interests.

- *Describe how you have worked through other people to accomplish something important.* If the candidate cannot answer this question convincingly, he or she has not accomplished much outside the realm of academics in terms of an ability to elicit aid or to persuade.

- *Describe a major risk you have taken in your life, beyond academics and the CPA exam.* The ability to deal with failure—and success—is a major factor in the ability to bring in business.

- *Describe two major successes in your life other than your scholastic success. How did you accomplish them?* Once again, look beyond the obvious to eliminate those candidates who are only good at one thing—studying and passing tests.

- *Describe how you recovered from an instance of personal rejection. How do you feel about risking personal rejection in your career in public accounting?* These related questions will reveal how the candidate views rejection. As mentioned earlier, it is best to ask these types of questions outside the formal office environment to elicit more candid responses.

- *Describe your decision-making process.* Only people who are comfortable with making decisions can help others make decisions and be successful at selling and marketing. If a candidate tells you that he or she has to mull everything over at length before coming to the best possible conclusion, chances are he or she will never bring in any work. Rainmakers do not necessarily make rash decisions, but they are comfortable with their decision-making processes and are able to reach conclusions quickly.

- *Describe how you creatively solved a problem for which there was no obvious solution.* Testing for creativity will help you avoid hiring those people who can think only in linear terms. If a candidate does not exhibit creativity, he or she will have a difficult time bringing in business. When dealing with people, there are rarely simple, straight-forward solutions.

- *What will you need to be satisfied in public accounting?* People who are easily satisfied, have simple goals, and do not want to venture beyond the familiar will never be self- motivated enough to take risks and bring in business.

- *What skills are most important to becoming successful as a CPA?* If the candidate does not see beyond the technical application of what he or she has learned, he or she may lack the insight or desire to be involved with people.

- *Describe your interest in the art of persuasion. Compared to other skills, how does it relate to a successful career as a CPA?* Those who have not thought or read about selling probably have no interest in the subject except what they will feign in order to get hired.

- *What have you accomplished as a leader? What role do you see leaders having in public accounting?* Hire leaders to ensure the future leadership of your firm. Hiring sheep or lemmings will lead to the firm's inevitable failure.

- *Describe the different kinds of people you have lived, studied, worked, and dealt with. How do you deal successfully with these different personality types?* Look for flexibility in dealing with other people before you hire.

- *What do you consider to be your strengths other than academic ability? Why are they important?* Stop hiring book-worms.

- *Describe how you feel about challenges outside your given strengths. Give an example of such a situation.* Hire people who have overcome adversity. These people have proven their ability to go the extra mile. Most will succeed despite the difficulties inherent in building a practice and being a CPA.

In this chapter, we have discussed how to hire the right people in the first place. The next four chapters will review how to develop the entrepreneurial spirit in the current members of your firm.

6

Developing Entrepreneurs—Emulating the Right Role Models

If you want to improve your golf game, would you rather talk to Jack Nicklaus or the average player? The same principle applies to developing the entrepreneurs currently on your firm's staff. The key is to have them emulate the behavior of those who are already successful at bringing in business.

Unfortunately, rainmakers are rarely able to describe how they built their practices. They usually say things like, "I just went out there and met people." or, "I just did it." One CPA, when asked how he built his firm into the second largest in a major city, said, "I stood in the hallway and shook hands."

Top business producers are models of success

Guide your staff members to emulate the behavior and thought processes of top business producers. Identify attributes of the top business producers to enable your staff members to guarantee their own success. Consider how rainmakers think and what they do, step by step, to build their practices. You will notice that these thought processes and activities are not what one would expect from a typical CPA.

How top business producers think

They work smarter   Do not misunderstand this thought process of the top business producers: It does not mean they work *harder*, it means they work *smarter*. Most successful business producers maintain their market presence every day of the year because people are always in the "buying cycle." The buying cycle ranges from "not interested" to "must buy it immediately."

Chrysler, AT&T, and other successful companies advertise and market to their prospective customers every day because they do not know when you will be at the "must buy" position, and they want to be right in front of your face the moment you get there. If they are not, you are likely to choose a competitor.

The same theory applies to the purchase of professional services by clients and prospective clients of CPA firms. Only accountants stop all activities other than getting out the work for three to five months each year. Over 90% of CPAs do no personal marketing during busy season. It is difficult to maintain a market presence when you take yourself out of the market for a certain time every year.

The top business producers in the accounting profession do something every day—even during busy season—to build their practices. Whether by meeting for lunch, breakfast, or drinks with a client, prospective client, or referral source; sending an article to someone; or making a phone call, these CPAs make some form of contact every single day. This is unlike most CPAs, who conduct such activities sporadically, if at all.

Working smarter does not mean spending your weekends and evenings at Chamber of Commerce meetings. However, many top business producers do mix social activities with business, killing the proverbial two birds with one stone.

That is working smarter. Rainmakers have made personal marketing a habit—they do it every day. Because they are always in the marketplace, when a prospective client or client needs their services or a referral source is in a position to refer, they are right there, fresh in people's minds.

"Many times I'll run into somebody at a social event and they'll say 'Steve, I was thinking about you. I need to call you about some tax advice and I'm glad I saw you. Let's get together next week to talk about it,'" says Steven Messing of KPMG Peat Marwick, Miami. "I would hate to think that if that person had not seen me, they wouldn't have called me, but it's probably true. When you are out of sight, you are out of mind. . . . You have to be seen by as many people as possible."

Also, working smarter means that top business producers see the business development implication in everything they do. They understand that they are always marketing.

Because so much of a CPA's new business must come from his or her existing clients and referral sources, rainmakers make an extra effort to remind themselves they are still in the "romance" stage of every professional relationship. Unlike most CPAs, who take their clients for granted and pay little attention to business relationships, entrepreneurs are constantly aware that everything they do affects these relationships. They understand that delivering and reviewing the audit report is marketing. They know that every contact they have with a client will bear upon that relationship in some way. They are constantly looking for opportunities to help their clients succeed.

Budding entrepreneurs must see the business development aspect in everything they do. The idea that the client pays their salaries must be conveyed in every staff and partner meeting. Also, staff members must emulate the top business producers by making business development and personal marketing a habit, even during the busiest and most important times of the year.

They always think about business development   Top business producers understand that building and keeping a practice is a game of analysis, strategy, and implementation, like chess. Like any game, the more you think about it and try to improve, the more successful you will become.

Unlike their competitors, entrepreneurs think about business development most of the time. Although the work needs to get out and they have other obligations and concerns in their lives, the thought of building and caring for their clients is foremost in their minds.

Rainmakers' antennae are always up. They have a nose for business. They are constantly thinking about business opportunities and new ways to win at their game. Because of this, they rarely miss opportunities that their competitors—who have their noses so deeply embedded in their daily work that they do not notice opportune moments—pass right by. From the time they wake up in the morning until the time they go to bed, entrepreneurs are playing and winning the game of business development.

My favorite example of this, although extreme, illustrates the point well. One of my clients is the managing partner of a very successful firm and for years has brought in the business that keeps the firm at the forefront in the marketplace despite tremendous competition. Because his antennae are always up, he closed an appointment that led to a sizable audit client—at his daughter's wedding! Standing in the receiving line greeting guests, this rainmaker met someone he did not know. After the introductions, the CPA asked his guest about herself.

In our culture it is perfectly acceptable to ask someone what they do for a living as a way of breaking the ice. Because he always thinks about business development, this CPA has made a habit of asking that question in every social situation—even his daughter's wedding. The guest replied that she owned a local business, and the entrepreneur took note. Later, while circulating among his guests, he made a point of stopping to talk with this new prospective client.

The CPA decided to allow eight minutes to make an appointment with the business owner, and not a minute longer. So he reintroduced himself and asked about the guest's business. When the eight minutes were up, the CPA said, "Did you know that I am the managing partner of the XYZ CPA firm here in town?"

Pay close attention to the way the CPA worded his question—it has helped him close much more than his share of business over the years. By focusing on business development, he has already thought about his phrasing and questioning, which are some of the tools of selling. He did not blurt out stale lines like "Can I call you for an appointment?" or "I'll be in your neighborhood. Would Tuesday at 9:00 or Thursday at 11:00 be better for you?"

Instead, he said, in the least threatening tone possible, "Should we be discussing your accounting work?"

Most people find this question to be to be nonthreatening because it starts with the word should, not can. It creates a team effort by using the word we. The CPA does not sound like he is begging for the business—the word talking creates a relationship. With one sentence, the rainmaker has caused the prospective client to think about her accounting work and the nature of her relationship with her current CPAs. Most people find it almost impossible to respond negatively to this question.

Are the members of your firm missing opportunities because they do not focus on business development? Are you missing a chance to develop entrepreneurs because you do not regularly hammer this idea home?

They pursue only golden opportunities   Unlike most CPAs, who will pursue any kind of business at all and then let the ball drop from their fingers because of poor follow-through, top business producers concentrate only on those opportunities they want and follow them meticulously and tenaciously until the sale is closed. Many CPAs wait for a client's call, even though they think they have a great shot at securing the work. Remember, follow through is your job.

This is true of referrals, too. CPAs cannot afford to be so busy that they do not follow through on referrals in time, if at all. CPAs are probably the most disciplined people in business about writing things down, yet they fail to use their calendars to track referrals and secure business. A well-organized calendar is a powerful business development tool.

When rainmakers lose opportunities they should have won, many continue marketing by putting lost prospects on the firm's mailing list or inviting them to the firm's functions and social events. This lets the prospective client know the firm still wants their business. In more than a few cases, the rainmaker will automatically pick up that lost opportunity because he or she is still marketing when the client realizes they made the wrong choice in CPA firms.

Similarly, sometimes all a firm must do to regain a lost client is allow the client who has left to save face when returning, listen intently to the client's reasons for leaving, and perhaps change partners or staff on the job. As one successful rainmaker puts it, "I continue to market to the firm's lost clients even if they weren't my own personally. I feel such situations are better than only pursuing cold leads and strangers because former clients are already familiar with our firm and may feel they have made a mistake."

Top business producers also track their ideas about marketing, client relationships, and selling. CPAs should set aside at least one page in their calendars to record their ideas for building and keeping their practices. This then becomes their personal marketing plan, and all they have to do is prioritize and implement these ideas.

Be sure that your staff members know what they should be looking for, not only that they are supposed to "bring in business." Teach them how to use a calendar effectively. Provide a time management course for them, or at least encourage them to take one. Also, be sure your firm keeps in contact with lost opportunities and lost clients.

They think like entrepreneurs—not accountants   Consider your most successful clients: Do they think and act like CPAs? Although many entrepreneurial business people could probably be more disciplined, most are successful specifically because they do not run their businesses like CPAs often do.

From my research on how CPA firms dealt with the recession during the late 1980s and early 1990s, I discovered that over 95% of CPA firms dealt with the recession by firing people and cutting costs. Less than 5% changed their marketing efforts or the way they interacted with their clients. My most successful clients, however, confronted the economic downturn by trimming costs and laying off their least important people in addition to pursuing new marketplaces, bringing out new products, offering new incentive programs, and even hiring more salespeople.

The biggest competition accountants have is other accountants. If a person wanted to how *not* to run a business, he or she might look first to the typical CPA firm for guidance. Because CPA firms are typically run like democracies, it becomes very difficult for them to take action quickly. CPAs tend to grieve over every dollar spent. They usually do not invest as much as they should in their businesses, often sucking it dry with partner distributions. Also, they tend to ignore their clients. If CPAs owned a football team, the owners would play the games to save on salaries. Successful clients, however, manage their business and their employees, keep their customers happy, and constantly seek new business.

Amazingly, some firms have fired their best business developers and client managers, but kept the technicians and thus lost clients. Keep in mind that technical people are important—somebody has to do the work. But top business producers see beyond the technical and have a quite different outlook on business from their fellow CPAs.

Entrepreneurial accountants see the long-term, overall picture for their firms. They are visionaries. They know where they want themselves and the firm to be in three or five years. On the other hand, most CPA firms do not have a business plan; some do not even have budgets.

Top producers look at more than the bottom line. Many of them know that once they pass breakeven, a lot of the new incremental business falls right to the bottom line. Some CPAs are intent on micromanaging the bottom line, creating a smaller practice in order to boost profits. When that happens, the firm loses market share, word-of-mouth advertising, and referrals. By failing to create the opportunities for the up-and-coming stars to stay with the firm and become partners and by over-managing the bottom line, firms can manage themselves out of business.

One CPA firm was intent on eliminating the administrative function of their ten-partner firm, thereby saving about $10,000 per partner. The partners' idea was to abolish the very department that had made their firm's success and growth possible by freeing them from the mundane details of the business—only to add a few bucks to their $250,000 average draws. This certainly does not seem like common sense, but I have discovered that with CPAs, common sense is not all that common.

Top business producers invest in themselves and their staff members. They know that to build their firms, they must provide the training and support for the people who must go to market.

Entrepreneurs also invest in their personal appearances, their collateral materials (such as stationery), and their offices, knowing that the impression they make affects clients', prospective clients', and referral sources' opinions of them and their abilities. Many CPAs who wonder why they cannot bring in business apparently have never looked in a mirror and asked themselves, "What does my prospective client want to see?"

Sadly, some firms skimp in other ways, damaging not only their business development efforts, but also the quality of their daily work. In too many accounting offices, there is poor lighting, depressing decor, and less equipment than there should be, all because the partners do not want to spend money. All of these issues affect the attitude of the firms' employees, the quality of the work they produce, and they way they interact with clients.

Top business producers are open-minded, not closed-minded like most CPAs. They look everywhere, at everything, for ideas on how to grow profitably. Top business producers delegate as much of the day-to-day accounting work as possible to free them to sell and take care of their clients and referral sources. They take time to properly train their staff so they do not have to be tied to their desks. They take risks, knowing that the greatest risk in building a practice is not venturing beyond their comfort level.

Stop focusing only on the bottom line. Plan the growth of your firm. Train your staff to sell and improve client relationships. Take more business risks. Always try to increase your firm's market share.

Consider the thought processes of the top business producers in the accounting profession discussed here. How are they different from those of most CPAs? These differences separates entrepreneurs from their less proactive competitors. Encourage your staff members to become more entrepreneurial by changing the way they think about business.

How top business producers build their practices

Consider the following activities of those partners and managers who bring in the most business. Help the members of your firm develop their entrepreneurial abilities by having them concentrate on the actions that will lead to faster business development success.

They select their targets   The top business producers in all of the professions tend to select their clients, rather than letting the marketplace rule them. One can attempt to appeal to a broad array of business, or one can limit his or her focus, making a directed effort, which is usually far more successful than the general approach.

Accounting is the last profession to specialize. Consider the medical and legal fields—these professions have indeed changed. If you had a back problem, you would go to an orthopedist, not a general practitioner. If an employee was suing your firm for sex discrimination, you would go to a labor attorney, not a general business attorney. So it is with all the other professions, except accounting.

However, there are some forward-thinking firms, such as Friedman, Eisenstein, Raemer & Schwartz (FERS), Chicago, which has totally reorganized along industry lines. This gives FERS a tremendous competitive edge over firms that are still organized around traditional A&A and tax functions.

Specialization gives FERS a leg up on the competition because the partners now know exactly where to devote the firm's time, effort, and energy in marketing and related activities. The firm can speak to prospective and existing clients as an expert in their industries, rather than as a generalist. It can train staff members in a very directed way, along industry lines, making them experts at an earlier stage in their careers. Also, this pattern of organization differentiates FERS from other firms that still seek every kind of business, even if they have no market penetration in a particular industry or specialty.

Unlike most of their individual counterparts, accounting's top business producers tend to have specialized their client base along industry or service lines, thereby deciding ahead of time who they want their clients to be. Have your staff members select an industry niche or specialty they want to become experts in. <u>Decide who you</u> <u>want your clients to be</u>—do not be a victim of the general marketplace.

They market to their existing clients   The most effective marketing mix is based on the following formula for new business:

- **Existing clients**   60%–70% of new business should come from existing clients purchasing additional services, both through new, nonattest services and their referrals.

- **Referrals** 20%–30% of new business should come from referral sources, people outside your client base who are in a position to send business your way. Referral sources include those who have traditionally been in a position to send CPAs business, like bankers, attorneys, and industry-specific sources such as sureties and bonding agents in the construction business. Make sure your firm's budding entrepreneurs do not ignore other, less obvious, sources like securities brokers, insurance salespeople, real estate agents, vendors, friends, family, and other accountants specializing in different niches, as well as their fellow employees.

- **New contacts** About 10% of new business should come from outside your firm's existing relationships.

Unfortunately, most CPAs tend to ignore marketing to their existing clients and referral sources and waste an inappropriate amount of resources marketing to those they will have the most difficulty attracting—total strangers. In one very successful 10-partner firm, each partner manages a pyramid of 17 people. This firm was started 25 years ago by a sole practitioner with no clients and no business. Today it grosses well over $10 million. The secret to this firm's success is that it markets to its clients and referral sources almost exclusively, and they spend 4% of the firm's gross revenues on marketing.

Basically, the firm invests this money and effort by entertaining and being with its existing clients and referral sources. When asked why he thought this approach worked, the managing partner replied, "Most CPA firms are too darn cheap to take care of their clients and those wonderful people who send them business. We treat our marketing as a fixed cost, just like rent. . . . By spending time and money on our clients and referral sources constantly, consistently, and continuously, we have secured relationships that our competition will never realize."

Teach your firm's business developers to devote their time, effort, and resources where they will achieve the greatest return: building their existing relationships with clients and referral sources.

They turn their clients into a sales force Most CPAs never approach their clients for referrals. Yet they are in the best position to hand-carry the good news about their CPAs to other prospective clients just like them.

In 1989 a national marketing organization surveyed over 100 clients of CPA firms nationwide, asking them, "Do you give your CPAs referrals?" Interestingly, 50% of the clients interviewed said yes, they did or had given their accountants referrals. The other 50% said no, they did not. The number one reason clients did not give their CPAs referrals: They did not know the CPA was looking for new business. In fact, many remarked that every time they talked to their CPA, he or she was very busy, sending the message that the firm was not available or looking for new business.

Your clients cannot help you unless they know what you want. Direct your staff members into new, assertive behavior by having them ask their clients for referrals.

They win the inside game   Top business producers pay attention to two sets of relationships their competitors often ignore or mishandle. Rainmakers are smart about winning the inside game with the people at their clients' and referral sources' offices and within their own firms.

CPAs usually have one person they deal with in a client's office, but there also tend to be subsidiary influencers who affect the total quality of the client relationship. Not only are these people sometimes in a position to refer business to their CPAs, but they are sometimes able to save the client if the primary contact leaves the client's business. Top business producers nurture these secondary relationships as carefully as the primary ones.

In contrast, most CPAs do not look beyond the controller, CFO, CEO, or owner. They expend all their efforts on one individual, and if they lose that relationship they can—and often do—lose the client's business altogether.

Top business producers also win the inside game in their own offices. CPAs are notoriously difficult employers and public accounting places high demands not only on employees' physical and mental makeup, but also on their families, especially during busy season. Worse, it seems the only time one hears feedback in a CPA firm is when something goes wrong.

Rainmakers acknowledge these basic facts of life in accounting and go many steps beyond typical CPA firm policies: They treat their employees with respect, generosity, and even affection. They create relationships with those who work directly and indirectly for them that inspire loyalty and devotion. They are much more flexible and logical in their dealings with their staff.

Recently I received a phone call from a marketing director at a client CPA firm. Although revenues were up a staggering 22% from the previous year after installing a marketing program and training staff members to carry it out, there was a problem. According to the marketing director, the managing partner was "reverting to being an accountant," destroying the morale of the people who had created the firm's growth!

The managing partner was once again making the kinds of arbitrary, thoughtless decisions CPAs tend to make regarding their staff members. For example, several employees had approached him about using a sick day when their children became too sick to attend school or daycare. The managing partner flatly refused their request. This was not an unreasonable request. This practice would have prevented the employees from having to lie about being sick to stay home with their children. Only someone inflexible and unaware of the importance of team morale to building a practice would deny such a petition.

John Johnson, son of a sharecropper born and raised in poverty in Arkansas City, Ark., and the multimillionaire genius who founded a publishing empire based on the first African-American directed publication, knows how to win the inside game. In the 1950s, Johnson was losing promising executives and staff members to other black-owned magazines. He knew he could not be successful without his people to support him, so he installed a chalkboard in his office, displayed so he saw it every day. On that chalkboard he wrote the names of the 30 or so key people he absolutely could not afford to lose.

Every day, Johnson would look at that board and ask himself, "What can I do to improve the relationship I have with one of these people? What can I do to make their life better?" From then on, Johnson never lost a single one of those employees to a competitor.

Perhaps the people around you are not motivated to become more entrepreneurial because you are not doing enough for them as human beings to make their lives easier and more enjoyable. Public accounting is not an easy ride, but it does not have to be miserable. Accounting's top business producers go out of their way to win the inside game.

Mike Dugan, managing partner of Dugan & Lopatka, Wheaton, Ill., is such a managing partner. Dugan uses the designation "Director of Joy," and takes it upon himself to ensure that his employees actually love what they do. He constantly seeks ways to make their jobs better and even fun.

By winning the inside game in their own offices, entrepreneurs have more freedom to do what is in their own best interests, and the firm's. Instead of only doing the bare minimum, their employees are more productive and take on additional responsibilities and challenges. Top business producers tend to have little turnover in their offices, leading to greater continuity and better service.

Also, entrepreneurs' employees usually know their personal goals. Staff members know their employer's philosophy on client service, the vital importance of new business, and often how much business he or she wants to generate each year. Because staff members have this information, they can help the business developer reach his or her goals, they can remind him or her of these goals, and they become part of a team effort.

People love to be on a team working toward a common goal. It makes their work lives that much more fun and rewarding. Gerald Greenwald, CEO of United Airlines, said of his learning experience at Chrysler, "I got my first real exposure to what happens when a large number of employees focus on one common goal. Once it starts, it is a steamroller to success."

However, staff members' goals must be consistent with yours. Do not believe for a second that your employees will get excited about helping you get rich. There must be rewards for them as well— and these rewards generally go beyond money.

Similarly, your clients and referral sources need to know your goals for your practice, as well as for their businesses. Then they can help you, and vice versa. Accounting's top business producers discuss their goals with clients and referral sources.

Have your employees nurture the relationships they have with their clients—without losing independence, of course. Make them very aware of the relationships they have with other members of the firm. Win the inside game in your own office by making your employees happier in their jobs, and they will become better business developers.

They build alliances with fewer but better referral sources   I always expected to find that the rainmakers in the accounting profession have many more referral sources than the typical CPA. In fact, the opposite is often the case. Top business producers tend to have fewer but more intense alliances with referral sources with whom they have developed a strong personal rapport, and who they have identified as being able to help build their practices.

Also, top business producers become close personal friends with their referral sources. They understand that the basis of business is relationships. More often than not, referrals are made on behalf of CPAs who are not technically exceptional, but superior in their relationships with the referrer.

To create these powerful and productive relationships, rainmakers typically identify a few people they want to be in referral relationships with and "romance" them over a long period of time until the relationship becomes productive and secure. One cannot devote this kind of time, effort, and energy to a legion of referrers.

Also, accounting's top business producers are judicious about monitoring the give and take in referral relationships. One CPA keeps a payback list on her computer and looks at it every week. When a relationship tilts against her—that is, more referrals are going out than coming in—she prints a hard copy of this list and sends it off to the referral source in question.

Have your staff members diagnose the quality of their current referral relationships. Guide them to create relationships with people who can help them directly. Teach them that creating productive relationships requires an investment of time, effort, and energy over an extended period of time.

They build their personal reputations through marketing to strangers   Top business producers usually address this aspect of practice building last on their lists of priorities. Early in their careers, rainmakers may devote a lot of time to speech making, article writing, and such, but most begin their careers by nurturing the relationships they have and building on them, rather than by marketing to strangers.

Some CPAs try to build their practices by becoming famous accountants, recognized for their extraordinary technical prowess, serving on technical committees and the like. However, such endeavors do not always pay off as planned because people tend to hire people they know, like, and trust. People outside the accounting profession often have a difficult time distinguishing or caring about technical prowess.

Make sure your employees are devoting their energies where they will pay off in business generated, unless you are specifically trying to bolster their professional reputations. Realize that furthering their technical careers may not generate the business you had hoped for.

They know how to sell   When all is said and done, accounting rainmakers can close the deal when the opportunity presents itself—they know how to sell. If they did not figure out how to sell by themselves, they made the effort to learn selling skills and continued to improve them because they realize that it is the most important task of a successful CPA. A CPA may be great technically, but if he or she has no clients to buy his or her services, it all goes for naught.

Make sure your firm's future rainmakers understand the importance of knowing how to sell effectively. Also, make sure they have the training necessary to develop effective selling skills.

This chapter reviewed the thoughts and behaviors of the prototype Accounting Entrepreneur. In the following chapters, you will learn more specific ideas to guide your staff members to utilize these thought processes and behaviors.

7

Developing Entrepreneurs—Guiding Rainmakers

There are numerous ways to encourage your employees to emulate the successful thought processes of the top business producers in accounting.

Make sure your employees do not take clients for granted

Staff accountants and technical partners have the easiest jobs in public accounting. They show up and there is work waiting for them. Very few CPAs give any thought to how that work gets there or what it takes, from a human point of view, to keep it coming in.

Future entrepreneurs must learn from the beginning of their careers who is putting the bread on the table. It is not the CPA, it is the client. This message must be driven home at every opportunity—in meetings, newsletters, informal communications, and even signs around the office. Do not bury it in the employee manual. Your employees must know that client relationships can be very fragile, and must never be taken for granted.

Today, accounting is an increasingly competitive profession. Clients are generally more sophisticated and less loyal. Therefore, client relationships are more fragile and CPAs must be more dedicated than ever to serving their clients.

Make staff members responsible for client relationships

In essence, your firm's clients are your staff members' clients. If your employees ever lose this perspective, client relationships will suffer. Your staff members must understand implicitly that clients are the firm's most important asset and they will be held liable for placing that asset in danger. Accordingly, let them know that they will be commended and compensated if they improve client relationships.

Many CPAs do not see themselves as having clients. At the very least, the partner or supervisor is the staff accountant's "internal client." A staff accountant exists within a CPA firm to make the partners' lives easier and more effective. Also, staff accountants must realize that they have counterparts in their clients offices who are their own "clients."

Give staff members the authority to build relationships with their client counterparts

At a recent Management of an Accounting Practice (MAP) conference, one managing partner told me that his firm absolutely forbade its staff members to interact with clients in any way outside the realm of getting the job done. His employees were not allowed to talk casually, eat lunch, or drink coffee with the client's employees.

The partner maintained that CPAs must always be independent, even to the point of not talking to clients, but the logic behind this policy was beyond me. I was not surprised to hear from one of his contemporaries at the conference that his firm had been dwindling for years and its best people had long since left.

Do not merely allow your staff members the freedom to get to know their client counterparts, encourage it. Although they must maintain objectivity, it is the technical quality of their work as well as the human relationship surrounding it that makes clients happy. You must eliminate technical expertise as the sole measure of success as a CPA, or your staff members will never become entrepreneurs or develop a client base.

Of course, some people are afraid to allow their employees to interact with clients because the staff members might steal a client. If you lose a client, it is your fault—not the staff member's or the client's. Although you must delegate work and some client responsibilities to staff members, you can never delegate total responsibility for client relationships.

Try to create an interlocking series of relationships with your clients. Too many clients are lost because CPAs refuse to see beyond the obvious and trust their employees with more responsibility and authority. Also, clients are lost because partners foolishly monopolize client relationships. When partners retire or die, clients should not be lost because a lack of a long-standing transfer of relationships. Partners cannot build their practices without freedom from the day-to-day number crunching, which is only possible if they bring other people into their relationships.

Make it a point to systematically introduce all of your staff members to your clients and referral sources. I will never forget the story related to me by a client who had recently acquired a publicly held company from a competitor. The business was started by the founder in the proverbial garage. He had nurtured and developed, eventually taking it public. Of course, the CPA firm had gone along for the ride.

Unfortunately, many firms take these inherited clients for granted and use them as training ground for their newest recruits. This particular firm felt it was solidly entrenched with the client and assigned a new staff member. The firm never made it a point to have their staff members meet the client's employees, certainly not the higher-ups.

One day during a board meeting, the CEO/founder got up to go to the washroom. On the way back he stopped at the water cooler, of which he still owned 53%. The junior accountants on the audit were taking a break and were standing around the water cooler. Because they were engrossed in their conversation and did not know the CEO/founder, he could not get past them to get a drink.

The client marched back into the board meeting and fired the CPA firm on the spot. "What do I need these people around for?" he said. "They don't even know who I am."

Is this just an outrageous story that could never happen to your firm? Remember, these kinds of occurrences are called yets—they have not happened to you or your firm yet.

Introduce your staff members to as many people as possible at the client. Show them off—let your pride in them and their abilities show. This will build your employees' self-esteem and pride in your firm, and enhance their performance and client relationships. Also, the new client contacts may know potential referral sources they would like to introduce to your firm.

Build your staff members' entrepreneurial attitudes and skills by allowing, encouraging, and expecting them to create and nurture relationships with their clients from the beginning of their careers.

Change your employees' career perspective

Your staff members must stop thinking of themselves as accountants—this has little or no value in the eyes of the client. Rather, they must see themselves as "business doctors."

For most successful business people, the most important, valuable thing in their lives is their business. They place this precious asset in their CPA's hands for guidance and care.

Of course, this is not what accounting programs teach CPAs, but it is what clients want from their accountants. Most clients are not CPAs; they know they lack of interest in matters relating to accounting.

Because of this, there is much more value in having clients perceive CPAs as business doctors. Of course, clients can only see us in this more highly valued way if we change our attitude toward them. This change in attitude requires that CPAs focus not on the daily grind, but on how we can help our clients be happier and more successful.

Fortunately for rainmakers, most CPAs are not willing to change their focus from being glorified—and expensive—bookkeepers. By helping your staff members see their roles as CPAs differently, without losing independence, you will help them become better business developers.

Do not promote nonproducers to the partnership

Recently I spoke with a managing partner whose firm had not experienced any top-line growth in the previous four years, though its costs had increased substantially. When asked what he was doing to change and improve the firm, he replied, "We'll be promoting Bill to the partnership in July." Upon further questioning about Bill's business development efforts, referral sources, and client relationships, the partner said, "Bill doesn't bring in any business to speak of." Bill was being promoted simply because he was "a wonderful accountant" and the firm was afraid to lose him.

No wonder the firm was going nowhere fast. The partners were still promoting technicians, thus sending the wrong message to every other member of the firm about what it really takes to succeed in public accounting today. The partners were afraid that Bill would leave and they would be stuck without his technical ability—which is far less salable than business development skills in a competitive market.

Consider why attorneys make so much more money than accountants. The reasons include the nature of the relationship attorneys are taught to have with their clients (to be the client's advocate) versus the relationship CPAs are taught (to be the client's accountant). Certainly, attorneys are taught a lot more about the importance of the power of persuasion (e.g., closing arguments) than CPAs. But most important, attorneys are much more successful than CPAs because they promote and compensate the right people.

Attorneys put people working in law firms into three categories—finders, minders, and grinders. The finders bring in business, and almost always make the most money. Minders nurture and take care of those vital client relationships to ensure the longevity of the client with the firm. Grinders are the technicians who actually do a lot of the work. The finders are the heros in the legal profession.

However, the grinders are the heros in the accounting profession. The technicians in CPA firms grind out the work and are paid handsomely on the basis of billable hours and collections, usually earning more than the finders who supply the firm's lifeblood.

Although many CPAs want to believe otherwise, there is very little minding done in the accounting profession. An annual client survey conducted by *CPA Profitability Monthly* (formerly *CPA Quality Client Service*) found that approximately 90% of the client relationships held by CPA firms are at risk, but the CPAs are not aware of a problem. In fact, given a better opportunity, 90% of the clients polled would switch CPA firms.

Technicians who have little desire or ability to be rainmakers must not dictate firms' policies. They typically do not understand or appreciate the effort involved in bringing in business and nurturing relationships. Technicians prevent rainmakers from earning what they should and doing what they must to build their practices. They have the wrong attitude toward investing in marketing and selling and can poison the business development efforts of the best firm.

Although your firm may sometimes have to promote a technician to the partnership to avoid losing an exceptional accountant, you do so at your own risk. If your firm does promote a technician, make sure that person is a partner in name only.

One of my clients decided to go a step further and split the rainmakers from the technicians to recreate the firm. The technicians were hindering the firm's business development effort and losing more than their share of clients. They were simply overpaid for pushing pencils. The firm polled all of its clients, asking if they wanted to go with the two rainmaking partners or with the three technical partners. Every "A" and "B" client, save two, chose to go with the rainmakers. The technicians left with practically nothing. In the first fiscal year ended after the split, revenues had jumped 18% over the previous year, with three fewer partners.

Another CPA firm went the other route. One partner had almost single-handedly built an eleven-partner firm of over 80 professionals. The firm dominated its marketplace, but the founder was 55 going on 75, he looked so tired. He was running himself ragged trying to keep the firm growing.

You see, he had hired and promoted technicians to the partnership. Of the other 10 equity partners, only one had the remotest interest in building the practice. Not only were the other partners not finders by nature, they were not minders either. All they did was grind away. The partners were mainly concerned with controlling the bottom line and had let the office go to hell, lost great employees, and focused on their pocketbooks instead of the big picture. Because the founder had lost control of the business by selling off his shares over the years, he was fighting a losing business development battle alone.

Because he was an entrepreneur, not a typical accountant, the founder knew that the firm was slowly going out of business. "We've got terminal cancer," he said sadly. When he retired, the firm did too—it was just a matter of time.

Do not let this happen to your firm. Deliver the message of nonpromotion of technicians loud and clear and often.

One 14-partner firm decided to take this advice. This new message was not buried in the employee manual, it was mentioned in every employee review and at monthly staff and manager meetings. This kind of repetition is necessary to ensure that your message is internalized.

One member of the firm, Diane, took this message seriously. She had always wanted to be a partner in the firm but had never really thought about developing her people skills, referral base, or selling skills. When the partners backed up their decision by promoting only those who demonstrated the ability to bring in business, Diane knew she had to become an entrepreneur.

Because Diane was a CPA with a powerful goal, she set about systematically building her practice. Using the training the firm had provided, she began methodically building a referral network, improving her client and referral source relationships, and selling.

In four years, Diane developed personal book of business from $0 to $500,000. She was rewarded by being elevated to the partnership.

Have staff members learn about clients' businesses on their own time

Your staff members should make an investment of their own time in their future success. Study does not have to be done on the firm's time. Your employees must contribute to their own success beyond the tens of thousands of dollars in training and educations the firm has already invested.

Clients appreciate dealing with someone who has expertise in their industry and who is familiar with the challenges and problems facing them. Most CPAs are still generalists, and their clients do not value their services as highly as they would a specialist's.

Make staff members responsible for reporting on the latest developments in a specific industry or profession. Have them make these reports at meetings within the firm. Put those who do the best job of studying and speaking on an industry directly in front of existing and prospective clients in that industry, either at a public seminar or at the client's office. These exercises will require your employees to learn the skills necessary to succeed in marketing and business development.

Also, note carefully those who do a poor job or is unwilling to invest their own time in learning about an industry. These people must never be allowed into the partnership.

Have staff members invest in their own people skills

This is a very effective way to separate those who are committed to the success of the firm and those who are not. People can always come up with excuses not to do something. However, when someone wants something badly enough, they will find a way to accomplish what they desire. Pay close attention to those people who will go the extra mile to improve their public persona through courses, public speaking groups, and leadership in organizations.

Suggest that staff members find mentors

Selling, business development, and the power of persuasion are the greatest skills in the world. Most CPAs believe that these skills intuitive. However, some have been fortunate enough to be shown the way by someone who already excels at business development and selling. Mentoring is an important way to enhance the learning process and push people beyond their fears.

Finding a mentor for staff members, however, is not the firm's job. If you are clear about what is required to succeed in your firm, mentoring should seem like a good way to help learn the necessary skills. If a mentor is not readily available within your firm, suggest that staff members look outside the firm in other professions or among their friends, relatives, and existing contacts. Have them look for someone who will act as their personal coach on a regular and continuing basis.

In this chapter, we reviewed numerous proven ways to change the way your staff members think and to have them emulate the top rainmakers in the accounting profession. In the next chapter, we will explore specific ways to modify your employees' behavior to help them be more entrepreneurial.

8

Developing Entrepreneurs—Encouraging Entrepreneurial Behavior

In this chapter, we will review proven and specific ways for you to propel the members of your firm into more entrepreneurial behaviors.

Have staff members join powerful organizations from the start

Most firms do not expect their staff members to do much outside the office during the first five years or so of their careers. Bright people are hired with all sorts of dreams and aspirations about their careers. They are impatient to get started in the real world because they have been stuck in school for most of their lives.

CPA firms, however, dismiss these desires and require them to apply all of their efforts to learning how to be good technical accountants, ignoring almost every other aspect of their careers. When staff members approach the level of manager or even partner, some firms divulge the fact that there is more to public accounting than technical work—there is business development.

Unfortunately, these people have not been systematically building their networks, getting their feet wet in leadership roles in their communities, or getting involved in the marketplace. They have no clue about selling and marketing, but the CPA firm sends them to market anyway. Then the partners complain that the staff members do not want to market and sell and are not motivated to build the practice.

CPAs must never take themselves out of the marketplace. They should begin nurturing their relationships from the very beginning of their careers.

Consider how your firm encourages such activities. Do not bury this idea in an employee manual that nobody reads or discuss it only in passing. Include this message in each of your firm's meetings, in the review process, in casual conversations, and in newsletters. To teach and motivate your staff members, the messages you send about business development must be constant and consistent or people will revert to their old, comfortable behaviors.

Keep in mind that your firm need not choose the organizations its employees join. Have staff members investigate five organizations and present suggestions for the two they should join and actively participate in. Have them prove to you which are most worth their time and will have the highest ultimate payoff.

Encourage your employees to stay in contact with classmates

If you lose touch with people you went to school with, it is difficult to pick up the relationship. Have each staff member create an inventory of their existing contacts without dismissing any as inconsequential. Staff members should prioritize each list according to the contacts' potential as a referral source and create a plan of action for staying in touch with the people on the list. This effort to improve and maintain their personal relationships can eventually lead to working referral relationships.

Most CPAs have lost track of past acquaintances who are now important in the community. It is never too late to begin this process of systematically identifying, prioritizing, and developing key relationships.

Hold staff members responsible for taking visible leadership roles

CPA firms should hire people who already have leadership and business experience. A former officer in a fraternity or sorority helped run a small business while he or she was in school. The president of a campus organization gained valuable leadership experience.

Unfortunately, CPA firms usually dissuade their staff members from taking visible leadership roles early in their careers, forfeiting potential referrals and slowing the staff members' development. Instead of worrying that junior staff members will somehow embarrass your firm, consider the positive effect their presence in the community will have on the firm's image. Your employees' ability and enthusiasm will demonstrate the firm's progressive attitude and its desire to return something to the community for all the benefits it has received.

CPAs are often invisible in their communities, unlike members of other professions. Doctors donate their time and attorneys do pro bono work, but CPAs tend to neglect the communities that support them. Perhaps this is because CPAs are not paid for these kinds of efforts and therefore cannot see the direct benefit of investing the time and effort necessary to make an impact in the communities. Yet the CPAs who are the most active in their communities generate the most referrals and new business.

Do not discourage your staff members from taking visible leadership roles early in their careers. Often, this is how non-CPAs judge accountants' ability and expertise.

Remember that people will live up—or down—to your expectations. If you expect your employees to hold community leadership roles, and this message is sent home early and often, your firm will gain a tremendous marketing advantage and make its staff members better leaders from day one. Likewise, if you expect staff members to devote a certain percentage of their free time to these kinds of activities from the beginning of their careers, you will not have to struggle later to get them out of the office and into the market.

Vote on outside activities

Your firm provides a lot of security for each employee. Therefore, in a more competitive environment, your employees should be expected to invest some of their own time and effort in improving and maintaining the firm—and their own future. One way to get this message across is to have staff members vote on how many hours a week they will devote to outside activities as their fair share. People usually resent something unless it is their own idea.

Of course, people will always find a handy excuse for not getting involved outside the nine-to-five grind. Consider holding outside involvement to a vote. A good starting point is two hours per week minimum away from the office on their own time for involvement in the community, doing personal marketing, and so on.

Two hours per week, of course, is over a hundred hours of free time over the course of a year. Multiply that by the number of people in your office and you many have a lot more personal marketing going on than ever before.

Delegate responsibility and authority for various administrative tasks

Give people administrative responsibility and authority early in their careers. This will boost their self-confidence and tie them into the firm in a way that enables them to take pride and ownership in working for your firm. Also, it will help develop their skills in managing and dealing with other people. The firm's partners, managers, or administrator need not be responsible for everything, nor do administrative duties have to be done only on firm time.

At a recent training program, my partner-contact complained about how much work it was to set the whole thing up. He had to check the partners' schedules, arrange a room, secure the proper audio-visual equipment, arrange for my travel plans, plan lunch, and so on. Instead, he could have assigned all these tasks to one or two staff members. None of the tasks were difficult enough to require the managing partner's personal involvement. All he needed to do was manage and support the staff members' efforts. The net result would have been that the partner's time would have been made available and one or two staff members would have had the responsibility and authority to carry out an important project. They would have felt proud of their efforts, grown in their roles as employees of the firm, and become less afraid to take risks and action because of it.

Take time to delegate administrative tasks to staff members when possible. You may be surprised by their responses, especially if you remember to praise and appreciate their efforts.

Host mixers with other professional firms

Many fraternities and sororities require their members to attend mixers designed to introduce them to new people. The members are, in essence, forced to meet people they otherwise might not have encountered on campus. CPA firms can do the same for their staff members by contacting local banks, law firms, securities firms, insurance agencies, bonding companies, or real estate offices and inviting them to a get-together.

These functions should be held frequently—once a year or once a quarter is not adequate. Do it every month, even twice a month. Encourage your staff members to meet potential referral sources and nurture those relationships in a social atmosphere, where people can be relaxed.

Guide staff members to become friends with their referral sources

"Some of the best friends I've made have come from business contacts," says Steven Messing, KPMG Peat Marwick, Miami. "That's one of the major benefits of this profession: The exposure that you get to such a diverse group of people who are respectable and bright. You really get a chance to meet a lot of quality people while practicing accounting.

"What's scary to think about is those situations where someone sees me socially or in public and says 'Steve, give me a call on Monday to discuss my estate.' What would've happened if I hadn't bumped into that person? Would I have missed getting the business? Would they have given it to my competition? That's also why it's important to turn your business contacts into your friends—you'll just see them more often and thus generate business you might not have."

The best referrals do not come from people who have a passing knowledge of what CPAs do. The kind of pre-sold situations that rainmakers love can only come from those people they have developed close relationships with, often beyond the typical business relationship. Encourage your staff members to make friends of their referral sources.

Give staff members time and money to invest

Another reason technicians out-earn rainmakers is that lunches with referral sources or clients and marketing activities take time away from the office and billable work. Often, business developers must pay for these activities out of their own pockets and out of their accrued vacation time.

No wonder people resent marketing. They have to pay for it themselves and the business they bring into the firm goes to the partners' economic benefit. Too many short-sighted firms dock their employees for taking extra time for lunches with prospective clients, and even make them pay for such lunches themselves.

Says Dan Fensin of Blackman Kallick Bartelstein, Chicago, "We give our people a monthly allowance to invest with their friends and contacts. We know that these kinds of meetings will eventually pay off in improved client and referral relationships and more business to the firm."

Encourage staff members to look for new ways to help clients

Help your employees keep their eyes open and think about how to benefit clients. Require them to present ideas for serving clients better or how clients can improve their businesses on a regular basis. Enforce this practice by designating a person to whom staff members should bring such ideas.

Of course, your firm's employees should already know that they are to bring new ideas for helping clients to management. However, this message must be constantly reinforced and staff members should be recognized and compensated for their ideas. Because most CPAs focus on getting the work out, they must be reminded to think about business development on a regular basis.

Set up a weekly Flash Report. Require staff members to give their ideas for serving the clients they are working with—or any client— to a designated person.

Expect staff members to bring in business from the start

Only your belief that junior staff members cannot bring in business will keep them from identifying opportunities and soliciting business from the beginning of their careers. Be clear about what you want and provide training to teach employees how they should accomplish this.

Have staff members develop an area of expertise

Allan Koltin, president of the Practice Development Institute and a partner with Friedman, Eisenstien, Raemer & Schwartz (FERS), Chicago, insists that accountants must change the way they do business in order to compete and succeed in the years ahead. In 1993, FERS reinvented itself along industry lines and has been even more successful because of the change. "The client perceives much higher value in the hiring process and in the relationship maintenance process when dealing with a specialist or an expert in their industry rather than a generalist," says Koltin.

According to Koltin, no firm is too small to create service niches.

"By being specific in the services and service lines you want to deliver, you can determine quite easily where to market your services."

To make entrepreneurs of your staff members, add spice and challenge to their careers, and further ensure their success, encourage them to develop an expertise or pursue a niche that they can market for the firm's benefit, and their own. Get some return on the investment of tens of thousands of dollars in time, effort, energy, write-offs, and mistakes your firm has made in every staff member. By developing a marketable expertise, your employees can not only return some of your investment, but also further their own careers.

Make each partner responsible for a specific industry or service specialty

Allan Koltin describes the reorganization process FERS went through: "As FERS matured, we were becoming more generalists, and having a tougher time managing the 'big blob' which our firm had become. . . . The impetus for change at FERS was an AICPA Group B advisory firm study. The common trend seen in our profession was a movement toward industry specialization.

"We know that other professions have successfully specialized for years. CPAs are the last to do so. . . . We surveyed the 100 largest CPA firms in the country and one trend was more apparent than any: The firms that had developed expertise in a specific industry or consulting arena and who had a champion for that practice area, an individual who was betting his or her career on the success of that practice area, were succeeding tremendously over firms who had not specialized."

In this chapter, we have reviewed many ways to have your staff members act like entrepreneurs. The following chapter will review the importance of accountability, support, and sales management.

9

Developing Entrepreneurs— Accountability, Support, and Management

One managing partner recently said of a fellow partner, "I can't understand why he isn't building his referral network. He won the silver medal when he took the exam! He should know better—he's a partner!"

Most teachers maintain that very few students would turn in their homework in the absence of some system of accountability. CPAs are the same way when it comes to business development. Left to their own devices, most will concentrate on the direct money-maker—grinding away—rather than on activities they would rather avoid.

Partners, managers, and staff members must be held responsible for business development

You will be pleasantly surprised by how people participate in business development when they are held accountable, preferably by a managing partner, partner, marketing director, or administrator with the necessary authority. Most of my clients have set up a simple penalty system: If business development reports are not turned in each month, the staff member is fined $50. It is amazing what only $50 will do to change someone's behavior!

Have department heads report on their progress regularly

It is vital to the growth of a practice and its staff that the people in charge of industry groups or specialized services update the rest of the firm on their progress (or lack thereof) on a quarterly basis. Being "put on the spot" in front of a group of people is a great growth experience. Not only will people improve their efforts and results knowing they will have to face the partners in this kind of setting, but it will expand their horizons of personal marketing as they become more comfortable with group presentations.

Create a sales management function

Less than 2% of professional firms have a control function to monitor and adjust their selling and personal marketing efforts. Most successful businesses have a sales manager or someone else charged with monitoring and managing their sales processes. Later in this chapter, we will discuss an excellent sales management system that you can install within your own firm, or use to enhance the one you already have. (See pages 70–74.)

Devote part of your training budget to marketing, selling, and client relationship development

Accountants are information junkies—the more they know and understand about something, the more comfortable they will be with it. This is similar to developing an expertise in municipal auditing or any specialty niche. If your staff members do not have business development acumen already, teach it to them.

"At Arthur Andersen, marketing is part of someone's training, just like technical skills," says Bill Pruitt, managing partner of the Miami Office. "We have ongoing marketing training. We employ monthly training sessions to seniors on up, just like monthly technical sessions. We supply the tools; it's up to them to carry their weight."

One reason you have less competition than you might think is that CPAs are notoriously cheap when it comes to training their employees in selling and marketing. Certainly, training is mandatory in all of the vital technical areas—which most of your clients could care less about and have little effect on your firm's top or bottom line. But when it comes to selling, marketing, or client relationship management, very few firms are willing to invest. Unfortunately, many CPAs think these soft areas are understood intuitively and do not require any specialized learning.

Recently, a CPA approached me at a state CPA society session. "Thank you so much for your AICPA 'I-Hate-Selling' tapes," she said. "As soon as I listened to them, I sold a $25,000 client I know I never would have sold before!" When I asked where she got the tapes, the CPA replied that her 12-partner, 40-professional firm had a set in its library.

"How many more sets has the firm bought as a result of your success?" I asked.

"One set is all we have," answered the CPA.

Only CPAs would invest in a single set of tapes for an entire firm. The fortieth person will get to listen to that one set by the year 2000, perhaps. Such limited access not only slows the initial dissemination of the information, but also precludes repeat learning and reinforcement.

Do not foolishly believe that a one-day seminar held years ago or a single set of training tapes will make a difference in your firm's business development effort. A change in behavior requires a constant influx and continual reinforcement of new information. Without this, people will go back to their old, stale behaviors.

Selling, personal marketing, and client relationship management are not topics that can be addressed once a year or every five years if you want the training to show results. Monthly training sessions are most effective for maintaining the enthusiasm and information input necessary for a change in behavior and improvement in performance.

Offer monetary incentives

Consider one fairly large firm that was having problems with business development. Some partners were bringing in business. But no matter how much they told the other staff members that it was important for them to bring in business, no one else was participating.

This situation can be explained in a number of ways. First, the firm's employees did not know how to build their networks, identify opportunities, close sales, or build and maintain client relationships. Second, there was no reinforcement for effort or results. Third, there was no sales management system. Finally, the firm offered no monetary incentives.

The partners explained their compensation philosophy as follows: "The carrot is partnership. Let them prove to us that they want to be partners by bringing in business!" Even though the staff members were aware of the partners' expectations, their business development effort was weak at best.

Everyone must know how they will benefit from bringing the firm business. This must be reinforced regularly and systematically or they will forget. It hurts morale to see just the partners get rich.

Many firms provide a monetary incentive for business development. This monetary incentive—which will not work independent of the other factors mentioned above—generally ranges from 10%–25% of fees paid by the client for a specific period of time, ranging from the first year to as long as the client and the service provider are with the firm.

Most firms offer such an incentive for the first year only, which I believe is a mistake. Staff members may think, "Why should the partners make money and not me after the first year?" Monetary incentives should be paid for the life of the client. This provides an ongoing motivator to the person continuing to receive bonus checks. Also, the person bringing in the business will have an incentive to ensure that their client is being treated properly by the firm, improving client service and relations.

Bonuses should be paid monthly, in a check separate from the staff members' regular salary. Any additional bookkeeping concerns are minimal compared to the business development benefits of this practice.

This incentive works best if compensation is paid immediately upon securing the client, rather than a year later based on collections, which is how most firms remunerate. Positive reinforcement needs to be immediate and regular to be most effective. A year is simply too long for most people to make or care about the connection.

Also, the person who brought in the business should not be penalized for write-downs and collection problems. One very successful CPA says it is the partner's fault if there are write-downs or collection problems. His firm pays bonuses based on what the job is estimated at initially; the bonuses increase it the fees go up.

Some firms, like Blackman Kallick Bartelstein, Chicago, pay a bonus based on introductions whether work is sold or not. "We give practice-sharing to everyone, not only for business brought in, but for merely introductions as well," says Dan Fensin, managing partner.

The great majority of firms really miss the boat on new business by not selling additional nonattest work to existing clients. This kind of business development effort is often overlooked, yet it is often the easiest work to sell because the client has already hired your firm, continues to rehire your firm, and has overcome the fear of doing business with your firm.

Worse yet, most firms do not compensate for the identification of opportunities to sell additional work to existing clients. Partners insist that staff members are supposed to do that automatically, but cannot explain why it is not being done. In many cases, lack of monetary incentive is actually an impediment to bringing in this kind of business. Don't your clients pay a commission on sales to people who have purchased from them before?

Having two people on the same job fighting over recognition for the sale of additional business should be your biggest problem. In this type of situation, do what your clients do—split the bonus.

Help staff members feel the success of selling

At every opportunity, drag your staff members—from the lowest level up—on sales calls and to marketing and networking events. Explain to your clients that you expose your junior staff members to high-level meetings at every opportunity as your firm's way of fostering their growth as professionals. Most clients appreciate and respect this practice. You must let your employees experience the thrill of victory to whet their appetites for more and to alleviate their fears of the unknown.

"Build a culture around the philosophy of proactive firm growth by showing people the value in selling, letting people know the benefits of the firm growing, and letting people feel the satisfaction of selling—not only intangibly 'feeling good' about it, but tangibly—by giving them some reward for doing it," says Fensin.

Encourage and allow for failure

Fear of failure pervades most CPA firms. It is a fact of the profession: Failed CPAs get sued. As a result, CPAs have a way of emphasizing failure strongly to ensure it never happens again that makes most people afraid to take any kind of risk.

I insist that my clients learn to be comfortable with and appreciate failure as it relates to business development. My CPA firm clients establish two types of awards to be handed out at monthly sales meetings: the "Go-Getter of the Month" and the "No-Getter of the Month." The "Go-Getter" awards personal marketing, sales activity, and results, while the "No-Getter" awards sales failures and mistakes—but it still rewards effort, not sloth.

This gets people to appreciate the lessons learned through failure by rewarding efforts that failed but were at least made. The idea is to applaud and laugh about failure; it changes the perception and fear of it that permeates CPA firms.

Another way to encourage constructive failure is to have your staff members set their goals for the number of clients, appointments and referrals they will *not* get in a month. Many years ago when I was first building my practice, I hired the best sales consultant I could find. His first suggestion to me was to set goals for the number of failures I would create in the each of the following months, not the number of successes. His rationale was that a novice like me would encounter much more rejection than acceptance. He was right.

I set a goal of 60 refusals for the first month, increasing it by 10 for each subsequent month. By the time I reached the month when 120 people were supposed to tell me no, I simply did not have time to play the game because I had too much business.

Help your staff members overcome the fear of failure and rejection by focusing them on activities that will guide them to increased activity and success.

Aim for early successes and small improvements

When guiding people into a new or uncomfortable behavior it is best to have them take "baby steps" at first. These small steps should then progress into endeavors that are more risky and more frequent.

Kate was a new partner in a 55-person firm. She had never shown any inclination toward marketing or bringing in business. I was hired to provide her firm a one-year training program. program.

At our first training session, I asked everyone to set goals for the number of people who would not do business with them, would not give them referrals, would not set appointments, and so on, in the following month. Kate set her goal for the first month at five rejections—a baby step indeed.

At our next session, Kate was appropriately proud. She had engaged in behavior—actively seeking referrals and new business—she never would have tried before because she was too afraid of failure. She had set a goal she knew she could accomplish, and she did.

The next month, Kathy set her goal at ten no's.

When I returned six weeks later, Kate was even happier. "I got my ten nos," she told the group, "And three yeses!" Because her goals were reasonable and designed to help her succeed, Kate had started bringing in business in a very short period of time, developing from a straight technician to a budding entrepreneur.

However, in some CPA firms, marketing means having staff members and managers make cold telephone calls off a list for two or three hours at a time. Not only is this the least likely way to drum up business, but is also resented and resisted by the people forced to make the calls. Instead of forcing them into uncomfortable, no-win situations, guide your staff members to become rainmakers by having them take progressive baby steps that are monitored and encouraged.

Every partner must be a sales manager

Each partner must realize that he or she is the sales manager for his or her team. It is every partner's responsibility to encourage the sales effort by recognizing success and failure. If you ignore your employees' activities, they will ignore marketing and selling. Sadly, most partners do not give their team members any kind of reinforcement, except when a mistake is made.

You must take the initiative within your group to motivate your staff members to become entrepreneurs by sitting down with them regularly and reviewing their progress. This is how sales managers deal with their salespeople. Of course, this requires an investment of time and effort, and most partners are simply too busy grinding away to manage their staff members properly. The more partners nurture their staff members and encourage them to take risks and learn new behavior, the better results their firms will see.

Make heroes of staff members who bring in business

Usually the only heroes in CPA firms are the grinders who bill the most hours. Often the business development achievements of those who bring in work are kept secret from the other members of the firm. This mentality must change if your staff members are ever to become rainmakers.

Applaud those who bring in business, mentioning their accomplishments in newsletters and memos and at partner and staff meetings. Make sure every partner knows who has had what business development success so they can individually congratulate that person. This type of publicity and positive feedback motivates people to keep going in the marketing and sales arena. "We try to make it known when there are successes in the office—especially if someone below the partner level has achieved a success in an introduction—and we play it up," says Fensin.

Make your firm's sales and marketing heroes the superstars of your sales meetings. Allow them to describe how they bagged the latest client or secured the referral or spotted the new project. When someone who has sold very little in the past makes a sale, make them "queen or king for a day" as well. Recognition, reinforcement, and praise will help your staff members grow into rainmakers.

Support your staff members in print

Assist your budding entrepreneurs with their personal marketing efforts by jump-starting their careers in the public domain. Instead of getting an article by your firm's tax hot-shot published, have a promising manager or staff members write the article. Not only will this kick off their personal marketing program in a powerful way, but it also shows that your firm cares enough about them to devote its resources to enhancing their personal reputation through community or industry exposure.

Ask future superstars to help struggling staff members

Partners are not the only effective mentors. Your firm's promising staff members can themselves benefit by mentoring others who want to improve. As the saying goes, the best way to learn something is to teach it.

Boost the self-esteem of those who show sales promise by having them work with others who have been hesitant to market and sell. Do not waste their time, however, on those who are resistant to change. Not everyone is rainmaker material; invest time and effort only in those who are interested and willing.

Do not accept any excuses—even during busy season

When it comes to finding excuses not to market or sell, CPAs may be the best. All too often, people hog work or do things they do not have to do because they only feel comfortable with familiar activities.

Stop accepting excuses! Send your employees to a time management training program and teach them how to prioritize and delegate. Develop their management skills so they can find the time to develop the practice.

Everyone has time to market and sell, even during busy season. If your staff members cannot find the time, remind them that they must make time for business development if they want to get ahead in the firm.

Tie compensation to business development

It is no surprise that there is little practice-building happening in most firms because the typical compensation system is tied to billings. Most firms do not include marketing activities as part of their annual compensation program. Business development must represent a certain percentage of one's salary increase in order for it to be taken seriously. Also, do not look only for "wins," but compensate for effort, especially that of junior staff members. Emphasize contact-making and follow-up activities. If your staff members are actively building their referral networks and identifying sales opportunities with existing clients, open up the checkbook and add to their normal salary increase accordingly.

One firm has compelled its partners to become entrepreneurs by eliminating the partners' participation in profit sharing if they do not actively market and sell. Another firm has created a $7,500 income allocation after partner salaries for only those partners who actively pursue and market their niches. The people who used to merely grind away are now actively pursuing their own self-determined niches and results are coming in like never before.

A third firm has changed its partner compensation program so that billings and collections represent only half of the partners' annual compensation. The other half is tied directly to new business brought in. The net result of this change in compensation was an increase of over 20% in new revenues the first year.

Free your firm's business producers from detail work

Count your blessings if you already have people who actively bring in business. Many firms penalize their business producers by not giving them the support they need to do what they do best—sell and market. Ask your rainmakers what they need and give it to them. Give those who are good at bringing in business the freedom to do so. Start running your practice like a successful business, not like an accounting firm.

Have partners lead the way

People are led by example. J. Paul Getty said, "Example is the best means to instruct or inspire others. The man who shows them as well as tells them is the one who gets the most from his subordinates."

"I think one of the key things in helping people develop skills where they will be able to market services is they have to be led by example," says Steven Messing of KPMG Peat Marwick, Miami. "They have to see the partners being out and about in the community, getting involved in organizations, and bringing in business themselves." Bill Pruitt, of Arthur Andersen's Miami office, agrees: "Competent people react to their perception of what's important to the leadership."

Partners must be actively and noticeably involved in the community, or staff members will think such activities are not part of their jobs, either. Partners must have excellent selling skills or future rainmakers will not try to develop those skills. Also, partners must be hungry for new business or staff members will not be hungry.

Do not expect your firm's staff members, managers, or partners to be out securing new business and meeting people if the firm's leaders are not personally doing the same thing. Everyone must participate in the practice development effort.

Install a sales management system that works

Amazingly, less than 2% of the CPA firms I have encountered have any form of regular sales meetings. Most successful businesses have monthly, or often weekly, sales meetings to keep everyone focused and to continue the learning process. Of course, most CPA firms do not want to have sales meetings because it takes up time that could be billed to their clients.

A consistent, monitored business development effort is more effective than one that runs in spurts. Keep the business development process focused on purposeful activity, not only results. Also, create and maintain a forum for discussion of business development problems and issues so everyone can focus on bringing in business and learn from each other.

The components of a successful sales management system include the following:

1. **Sales reporting system**   Although CPA firms are already overburdened with paperwork, there appears to be no other way to monitor activities effectively than through a simplified reporting system. This reporting mechanism is designed to hold people accountable for business development efforts, manage the process, monitor meaningful activities, and weed out the extraneous information that often accompanies such reports.

   This reporting system will help your firm manage its client relationships more effectively. It details what is going on with clients—information might not have known before.

   The main element of this system is a Sales Management Position Report. Filled out monthly by all partners, managers, and staff, this report summarizes the month's meaningful events, such as:

   • Work that is sold or lost

   • Sales that are still being closed

   • Referrals received

   These monthly reports are submitted to the managing partner, another responsible partner, or to the director of marketing. (See Exhibit 9-1).

2. **Monthly sales meetings**   These meetings are designed to create a free-flowing discussion meant to provide reinforcement, help close business, promote failure, facilitate peer pressure, and encourage participation and interactive coaching by the managing partner, the other partners, and the staff. Meetings are run by the

Exhibit 9-1

MONTHLY MARKETING REPORT

Name: _____

Month: _____

WINS: Anything positive—includes existing client activity as well as prospective business.

Name	Amount	Why

LOSSES: Anything negative—includes existing client activity as well as prospective business.

Name	Amount	Why

REFERRALS: Current activity from your referral ledger.
Received:

Name	Who From	Value	Notes

Given:

Name	Who From	Value	Notes

LEADS: Leads given/received from other members of the firm.
For others:

Name	Who To	Circumstances

From others:

Name	Who To	Circumstances

SALES/PROJECT IN PROCESS: Including new activities with existing clients as well as prospective clients.

Name	Project	Why Not Closed	Next Step

participants. However, it helps to follow an agenda that emulates the Sales Management Position Reports. (See Exhibit 9-2.)

Key points to remember when running a sales meeting include:

- **Provide reinforcement** Let people brag about their wins and share their losses.

- **Help close business** The group can often provide valuable input to the person who is stuck in a deal he or she cannot close. Such brainstorming exercises are learning experiences for everyone present.

Exhibit 9-2
Agenda for Sales Management Meetings
(One to Two Hours Monthly)

✓ Examine "Wins":
- Review details of situation (who, what, when, etc.)
- What worked?
- What didn't work?

✓ Examine "Losses":
- Review details of situation (who, what, when, etc.)
- What worked?
- What didn't work?
- Why was the business *really* lost?

✓ Examine "In Process":
- Review details of situation (who, what, when, etc.)
- Why isn't the business closed yet?
- What needs to be done to close the business?
- Requests for input from group and feedback

✓ Examine "Referrals and New Leads":
- Review details of situation (who, what, when, etc.)
- What worked?
- What didn't work?

- **Exert peer pressure** Partners should notice who is interested and participating at these meetings and who is not. Reward those who are active; deal with those who are not by discussing and breaking through their excuses in a one-on-one meeting.

- **Promote failure** It is important to keep the managers, staff, and partners aware that failure is acceptable. Without permission to fail, people will stop trying for fear of being ostracized. The less fear of failure, the more activity generated.

- **Examine wins and losses** By analyzing what went wrong in a sale, and what went right, everyone can learn from the situation. Exploring sales failures can take the pressure off of the person who did not make the sale. This is infinitely more productive than berating someone for losing a sale.

3. **Client service team meetings** Hold biannual client service team meetings in May and October to do a thorough review the health of major client relationships, additional work to sell, and any other items that come up. This is how major accounts are managed in traditional businesses.

   Participants must leave these meetings with plans of action. All members of the client service teams must participate, especially seniors and staff members because they are on the front lines.

The sales management process is not an easy one, but is the best way to ensure that the firm's environment changes to build entrepreneurs consistently over time. It is imperative that the process be monitored so successes and failures can be examined, celebrated, and learned from.

Although managing and controlling the process can be time-consuming, often the hardest part of business development is staying motivated. The final chapter will discuss that challenge.

10

Motivating People to Action

All too often firms lose their bright young superstars—the future rainmakers and partners—because the typical accounting firm environment is inherently wrong for promoting the entrepreneurial spirit. Firms often lose people when they could have been kept quite easily if certain policies had been in place. Amazingly, partners in some firms frequently do not know who the up-and-coming employees are. They do not discover that there is a serious problem with an employee until that person gives notice.

Most accountants will dismiss the following ideas for keeping good people, attracting better ones, and ensuring the future success of their firms as impractical or inappropriate for an accounting firm. However, all of these ideas have worked in accounting firms and traditional businesses. They require change, which is often difficult in businesses run like democracies so that every partner, no matter how backwards, has a vote. But the firms that have changed are now far ahead of their competitors.

Put yourself in your staff members' shoes

This is the most obvious way to improve morale and motivate people. Unfortunately, most CPAs treat their employees as they themselves were treated when growing up in the profession. However, times have definitely changed. Accounting firms, like sports teams, can no longer treat their young stars as they once did.

Many people ask me how I motivate my own staff. Every December, I ask each staff member to submit a written proposal regarding what will motivate them during the next year to help us reach our goals.

In their proposals, staff members discuss their accomplishments and shortcomings, as well as how we as a firm are better off than we were a year ago because of their participation in the team effort. This section must be very specific and should mention a heck of a lot more than merely getting the work out.

You see, most CPAs spend an inordinate amount of time trying to figure out how to motivate people, when the people themselves are the best judges of that. As for the concern that staff members will ask for the moon and the stars, consider that if CPA firms stopped pinching pennies they would be a lot more successful. Too many firms are penny wise and pound foolish.

Recently a CPA firm lost its brightest manager, the one person who could have been the future managing partner and main rainmaker, because the partners were not willing to match an unsolicited offer of 10% more in salary from a competing firm. It will cost the firm much more to find, train, and supervise a replacement, and the chances of finding someone half as good are remote at best.

So ask your how they want to be motivated. Perhaps they want an extra week of vacation when the firm, their team, or the individual reaches a certain goal. Maybe a new parent would like to apply his or her sick days to child care. Maybe they would like a dollar bonus if they reach a certain goal.

None of these desires is unreasonable or potentially detrimental to the firm. Instead of being inflexibly focused on the almighty dollar, consider how successful a firm full of effective, motivated people can be.

Create goals as a team

Every December the members of my firm sit down as a team and create our goal for the annual increase of fees the following year. Then we post the goal in the coffee room on a big piece of easel paper. At the top of the paper we write the amount of next year's increase in business. As we bring in new clients and sell additional business to our existing clients, we post those amounts on the chart.

Because it is in a main traffic area, members of the firm see this chart several times a day. As the firm brings in more business, they see the goal—and their bonuses, which are contingent upon achieving the goal—becoming a reality.

Each year since its inception, this practice has resulted in the firm reaching its goal before the end of the year.

Communicate about what is going on in the firm

People have a natural interest in their place of business. What you do with your business affects your employees both directly and indirectly. All too often partners see their firms as their concern and no one else's.

Many very successful firms let their employees know what is going on at regular intervals. If things are going well, the staff will feel secure. If things are not going as well as they might, the members of the firm can be called upon to help the cause by identifying more opportunities and securing more referrals.

Compensate for additional business and introductions

Compensate for business opportunities identified and sold to existing clients. Most accounting firms insist on compensating only for work sold to nonclients. If you buy a suit from someone in a store, the sales person will also receive a commission on any subsequent purchase you make. Likewise, the insurance person who sells you an annuity receives credit for later selling you a life insurance policy. Apparently, people in the retail and insurance industries know more about motivating people to sell than CPAs.

Similarly, compensate staff members for introductions to prospective clients, perhaps in the form of a $50 bonus. Remember, that kind of direct marketing is expensive, and you could advertise for years before a prospect decides to talk to you.

Too many accountants refuse to part with a little extra cash now and then to motivate people. They are their own worst enemies when it comes to motivating people and keeping the good ones.

Consider the firms that operate on a bonus point system as a way of motivating staff members. Employees earn five points for a new client, three points for a referral, and so on. If a staff member earns a certain number of points over a certain period of time, they get something. But if they do not reach that level, they get nothing. All of that effort goes for naught.

Forget the bonus point approach and motivate people by compensating for action immediately, the next payday, in a separate check. Reinforcement must be immediate and positive to work best.

Compensate for unsolicited comments about employees from clients

One way to quickly turn around morale is to let the members of your firm know that they will receive a bonus if a client of prospect makes a positive unsolicited comment about them (perhaps $25 paid in a separate check).

One CPA firm decided to try this practice because morale was quite sour. The first month, the firm decided to give an invented bonus to everyone (the comments were kept "anonymous"). Every staff member received a client comment bonus. A memo listing these bonuses was sent to each employee and an announcement was made at the staff meeting. The list was posted in the coffee room for everyone to see and the employees' names were mentioned in the firm newsletter. Checks were then handed out ceremoniously.

The next month, no bonuses were invented, nor did they need to be. A new level of service had been created because the staff members knew there was something in it directly for them. Employee morale went up until the partners decided to stop the bonus system because they had no time to write checks during busy season, when they were needed most.

For this kind of bonus system to work, it must be kept in place. Too many CPA firms consider only the money going out in bonuses, instead of taking into the account the increase in revenues better morale generates.

Clarify what it takes to succeed

Sometimes CPA firms survey their staff members to find out what it would take to improve the relationship between the owners and the employees. One of the most common responses is that it is unclear what it takes to succeed in the firm and where the individual stands.

Good people leave because they do not know where they fit in to the firm's future. Because of this lack of information, they go somewhere they can get a clearer picture.

Promote failure

Most members of accounting firms are scared to death to make the slightest mistake because they know they will never hear the end of it. To encourage your staff members to succeed, you must remove the fear of failure regarding practice development.

Help them set their goals for nos as well as yeses. Make a big deal over the person who asks for the most referrals in a month and gets the least. Give a bonus for the No-Getter of the Month. By motivating the right activity, people overcome their fear of rejection and adopt the behaviors necessary to be successful.

Give staff members marketing expense allowances

Staff members should not be expected to nurture their personal relationships and become rainmakers on their own funds. Some firms give their employees an allowance of $25 a month to take people they know to lunch so they can build relationships with them. By allocating a monthly allowance that is lost if not used, regular activity is institutionalized.

Give staff members their own business cards

Most CPA firms do not give their employees business cards, yet expect them to be making contacts. Business cards have a great effect on staff members' morale, making them feel like part of the team. Also, business cards are the cheapest form of advertising.

Allow your employees to help run the business

All too often, partners try to run the business by themselves and then complain they have no time to market and sell. Allowing staff members to participate in management gives them a vested interest in the future of the firm. It makes them feel more important because the firm trusts them to get things done.

One of Britain's most successful regional accounting firms had its managers create the coming year's business plan for the firm. The managers were excited and proud that the partners had entrusted them with this important job.

Motivate your employees by expanding the practice

Stagnant practices send only one message to their up-and-coming staff members: Someone will have to die or retire for you to advance in the firm. No wonder the best people leave—they do not see a future with a stale firm.

Usually those people who are not going anywhere stay with firms that are not going anywhere, either. Often firms lose the keepers and keep the losers because the partners are too busy grinding away in their offices instead of marketing to create space for the firm's future leaders.

All partners must commit to keeping the firm's stars

Recently a young CPA asked me if all CPA firms are alike—is it normal for partners to fight on a regular basis over their own personal turf? All too often, partners focus only on their own personal book of business and their own personal take from the firm. Accountants have never been known for having a global perspective, and this type of narrow vision comes to fruition to the harm of every member of the firm. Instead of working as a team, CPAs often work against each other, harming the firm, its developing entrepreneurs, and the client services it provides.

This attitude of self-protection and general lack of communication in most CPA firms was displayed recently by a firm on the west coast. At the first partners' meeting I attended, it was accidentally disclosed that Rita was leaving the firm on Monday. The partners were very distressed by this news. Rita was fantastic with the clients—they loved her. The reason she had given for her departure was that she did not feel she was appreciated by the partners or had a future with the firm.

Sadly, CPA firms lose their best employees for all these reasons, and because no one knows how the staff members feel about the firm and their roles in it. Certainly, a supervisor may have a vague idea that a particular staff member is generally unhappy, but he or she will often say nothing until it is too late to rectify the situation and the employee is gone.

The firm's partners must discuss their young superstars. They must abandon their stale old ways of doing business and create an individual relationship with each promising staff member. By opening up lines of communication and letting those people know there is a solid future with the firm for them, they will feel appreciated and like part of the firm's family.

Have every staff member make a personal marketing plan

It seems that CPAs need a plan of action to do almost everything; they need structure to maximize their effectiveness. Without a personal marketing plan detailing monthly activities and commitments to action, CPAs will never be as effective as they could be.

Make sure someone is watching

Somebody has to manage the business development process. Some person with the authority to reward and penalize must monitor the firm's monthly activities or little will be accomplished, except by those who have been self-motivated all along. Also, everyone needs to know who is not pulling his or her weight, as well as who is. (See Chapter 9 for further discussion of the sales management function.)

Tie compensation increases to personal marketing

All too often, firms wonder why their employees do not engage in personal marketing and entrepreneurial behavior. Yet, annual increases in salary are not related to the behavior firms want to encourage.

A portion of each annual salary increase must be tied to the expected behavior, or little will happen. Perhaps 50% should be allocated to personal marketing activities to catch your staff members' attention.

Stop criticizing, condemning, and complaining

Be more constructive in your criticism. Time and again, internal staff surveys reveal that staff members would like helpful guidance, not just criticism.

Praise every improvement

People will change in small increments. Make sure that every step is noticed and applauded. This requires an investment of time and effort, as does all worthwhile management.

Remember that negative reinforcement and management by fear and threat motivate only to the extent of the minimum performance necessary to avoid criticism. Positive reinforcement, however, motivates staff members to perform to their potential.

Demonstrate that not only the partners benefit

Nothing is more discouraging to budding entrepreneurs than seeing increases in business or profitability affecting only the partners' pocketbooks. People must see some personal benefit from their hard work or they will not be motivated to perform.

I am amazed at some of the environments that people work within. Many accounting offices are very cramped and have poor lighting. In some firms, people work with outdated computers, or even without computers or laser printers. Such firms make it more difficult for their employees to enjoy their work and, therefore, maintain a good attitude about the firm.

Many people do not produce the way they could because the partners insist on sucking every available dollar out of the firm, instead of improving the office environment and offering training and generally making superior performance possible.

Make heroes of budding rainmakers

If you have budding rainmakers, they must become the firm's stars, instead of the number-crunchers. Devote attention to these people because positive reinforcement is vital to encouraging their efforts. Others may resent this new attention to those bringing in the business, but perhaps it will give them an incentive to start marketing, too.

Manage the people in your pyramid

Partners are responsible for the business and personal development of the people within their own pyramids of influence; they are the firm's sales managers. Sales managers monitor the activities and growth of the people under them in the company's structure. They meet with their employees regularly, discuss marketing and selling, and provide the kind of personal attention that keeps the entrepreneurs growing.

Take staff members everywhere

I will always be grateful to the firm I started out with in public accounting. It was successful because the partners placed so much emphasis on developing their employees. They took me with them on sales calls, networking events, client meetings, and so on. In the beginning, they would usually tell me to be quiet and take notes. As time went on, they allowed me to take a more active role, helping me develop my skills in selling, marketing, and client relations.

Earn your employees' respect

None of the ideas in this book will work if people do not respect your and want to help you. So you and your fellow partners must remove yourselves from your ivory towers and start getting to know your employees on a more personal level.

Change partners' compensation

Everything discussed here must be applied to the partners. Partners need accountability and reinforcement—positive and negative—for their efforts just like staff members. But the best way to change behavior and develop entrepreneurial partners is by hitting them where it hurts and where accountants feel it the most—in the wallet!

Provide training for your employees

Selling is the greatest skill in the world, yet CPAs expect their staff members to do it without learning how. In order for people to become rainmakers, they must be continually trained in selling and marketing. Usually this expertise is not available within the firm, so it should be purchased through the local state society or an independent consultant. Amazingly, some firms send one person to a training seminar and expect that person to "borrow" copyrighted material and train the other members of the firm.

Change is the key

Everything discussed in this book requires one thing—change. This is both good news and bad news for CPA firms. It is bad news in the sense that most accountants do not like change and are suspicious and critical of change in general. It is good news in that your competitors do not like change either, and most are asleep at the business development wheel.

Changing behavior requires an infusion of information about the correct behavior and a consistent effort to modify the current behavior. Building entrepreneurs is a process, not an event. You cannot implement only one of these ideas and expect permanent, effective change to occur.

You will face an uphill battle when attempting to change your firm. You will have to fight those who are against change, those who are spoiled and comfortable in their jobs and careers. These people are like a cancer that slowly kills the organization, preventing it from progressing and changing to meet the new challenges of a competitive environment.

When fighting this never-ending battle and managing this continuous process, it may help you to keep in mind Richard Nixon's words to a man who was facing a great challenge in his own life: "A man is not defeated when he loses, he's defeated when he quits."

Action Plan

Steps to Take to Change the Culture in Your Firm

Hiring entrepreneurs

1. Have effective business producers conduct key interviews.
2. Be direct with prospective employees. Explain that every employee is responsible for building the firm's business.
3. Invest time in the interviewing process.
4. Take your candidates to a different environment, for example, to a casual social setting, to see how they interact with other people.
5. Hire people who have people-related experiences and are immediately likable.

Emulating the right role models

1. Encourage your staff members to emulate the thought processes of the top business producers in the professions, for example:

   a. Work smarter, not harder.

   b. Never stop thinking about business development.

   c. Pursue only golden opportunities and follow through until the sale is closed.

   d. Think like an entrepreneur, not an accountant.

2. Teach your staff members to devote their time, effort, and resources where they will most likely get the fastest return: building their relationships with clients and referral sources.
3. Institute custom-designed rewards for nonpartners to motivate them to help build your business. Ask them what it will take to motivate them to actively market and sell.

Guiding rainmakers

1. Make your staff members responsible for client relationships.
2. Have your staff members find their own personal sales mentors.

3. Introduce and show off your staff members to your clients.
4. Reinforce over and over to your staff members that in order to get ahead, they must build their own book of business.
5. Do not promote nonproducers to the partnership.
6. Encourage staff members to read industry journals on their own time.
7. Suggest that staff members invest in their own people skills.

Encouraging entrepreneurial behavior

1. Guide your staff members to identify, join, and take active and visible positions in organizations that include their counterparts in other professions as well as prospective clients.
2. Delegate responsibility and authority for various administrative tasks.
3. Encourage your staff members to turn their professional counterparts into their friends.
4. Expect your staff members to bring in business from the beginning of their careers.
5. Direct your professionals to develop expertise that they can then market for the firm.
7. Make each partner responsible for a specific industry or service specialty.

Accountability, support, and management

1. Have partners and department heads report on their progress regularly.
2. Devote part of your training budget to marketing, selling, and client relationship development.
3. Institute monthly training sessions to maintain enthusiasm and increase knowledge.
4. Tell everyone on a regular basis what's in it for them if they help build the firm.
5. Adjust your monetary incentives so that your staff members are compensated for business brought in for as long as they—and the client—are with the firm.

6. Make personal marketing, selling, client relationship management, and organizational involvement a material portion of your staff's annual salary review and increase.

7. Take your staff members everywhere, and put them into sales and marketing situations. Show them how it should be done.

8. Promote, allow, and reward sales and marketing failure.

9. Recognize and praise early successes and small improvements.

10. Make heroes out of staff members who bring in business and make contacts.

11. Help your staff members build their reputations and confidence by publishing articles about them and by them and by securing speaking engagements for them.

12. Do not accept any excuses for not marketing or selling—even during busy season.

13. Tie the partners' compensation structure to business development.

14. Reallocate resources to give your firm's rainmakers support staff, thereby freeing them from administrative work and allowing them more time to bring in business.

15. Institute a sales management system, including the monthly marketing report (see Exhibit 9-1).

16. Hold monthly sales meetings (see Exhibit 9-2).

17. Hold biannual client service team meetings for your major clients directed toward improving the client relationship, selling more work, and helping the client be more successful.

Motivating people to action

1. Identify your future rainmakers and commit to keeping and nurturing them.

2. Create firmwide and/or team goals.

3. Find out from your staff what it will take to motivate each one of them individually to help the firm reach its goals.

4. Treat your employees the way they want to be treated.

5. Post your goal for increased new business on an easily visible sign in a main traffic area.

6. Let people know what's happening in the firm.

7. Compensate for work sold to existing clients and for introductions.

8. Compensate for unsolicited comments about employees from clients and nonclients.

9. Let staff members know exactly where they are in the scheme of things and specifically what it takes to move to the next level.

10. Have your staff members set personal marketing and sales goals for "no's" as well as "yeses."

11. Give your staff members marketing expense allowances.

12. Assign administrative functions to staff members and allow them to help you run the business.

13. Require every staff member to have a personal marketing plan.

14. Invest some of your profits back into the firm in the form of improved working conditions.

15. You must improve your personal relationships with your staff because none of this will work unless they like, trust, and respect you.

16. Purchase business development training for your employees.

Self-Study CPE Program

Thank you for choosing this self-study CPE program from Harcourt Brace Professional Publishing. Our goal is to provide you with the clearest, most concise, and most up-to-date information to help further your professional development, as well as the most convenient method to help you satisfy your continuing professional education obligations.

The *Building Entrepreneurial People CPE Program* is intended to be used in conjunction with the Executive Report *Building Entrepreneurial People*. This course has the following characteristics:

Prerequisites: None

Recommended CPE Credits: 4

Level of Knowledge: Basic

Field of Study: Management

Harcourt Brace Professional Publishing is registered with the National Association of State Boards of Accountancy (NASBA) as a sponsor of continuing professional education on the National Registry of CPE Sponsors. Harcourt Brace Professional Publishing is recognized as a provider of continuing professional education by all state boards of accountancy except North Carolina and Mississippi. The Self-Study CPE Program is designed to provide four (4) hours of CPE credit if the test is submitted for grading and earns a passing score. Credit hours are recommended in accordance with the Statement on Standards for Formal Continuing Professional Education (CPE) Programs, published by the AICPA. CPE requirements vary from state to state. Your state board is the final authority for the number of credit hours allowed for a particular program, as well as the classification of courses, under its specific licensing requirement. Contact your State Board of Accountancy for information concerning your state's requirements as to the number of CPE credit hours you must earn and the acceptable fields of study.

To receive credit, complete the course according to the instructions. This four-unit CPE Program costs $39. Options for method of payment are shown on the answer sheet. If you would like to order additional CPE subscriptions for colleagues, you can do so by copying the blank CPE answer sheet and specifying the $39 method of payment for each order.

Each CPE test is graded within two weeks of its receipt. A passing score is 70% or above. Participants who pass the test will receive a Certificate of Completion to acknowledge their achievement.

Instructions for Taking This Course

1. Read the Executive Report *Building Entrepreneurial People.*
2. Take the examination, writing the letter of your answer on the corresponding line on the answer sheet.
3. When you have completed the examination, remove the answer sheet, fill in your personal information, specify method of payment, place it in a stamped envelope, and send it to the following address. (Please do not send CPE answer sheets to any other Harcourt Brace address.)

Executive Report CPE Coordinator
Harcourt Brace Professional Publishing
525 B Street, Suite 1900
San Diego, CA 92101-4495

Subscription information: If you would like to order multiple CPE subscriptions for colleagues, you can do so by copying the blank answer sheet and completing each card, with method of payment specified for each test.

To order the Executive Report *Building Entrepreneurial People,* call our toll-free number or write to the customer service address* (shown below) and give the product numbers 0-15-601712-1 for the *CPE Program* and 0-15-602419-5 for the Executive Report.

Harcourt Brace Professional Publishing
Order Fulfillment
6277 Sea Harbor Drive
Orlando, FL 32821-9816
(800) 831-7799

Note: This is a customer service address only; do not use this address to remit CPE answer sheets. For the correct address, see the "Instructions" section above.

Registered with the National Association of Stat Boards of Accountancy as a sponsor of continuing professional education on the National Registry of CPE Sponsors. State boards of accountancy have final authority on the acceptance of individual courses. Complaints regarding registered sponsors may be addressed to NASBA, 380 Lexington Avenue, New York, NY 10168-00092, (212) 490-3868.

Objectives

The CPE examination is intended to test your understanding of the material discussed in this Executive Report. When you finish, you should have a clear understanding of the following:

- Why CPAs are reluctant entrepreneurs
- How to overcome obstacles to effective business development
- Four ways to develop entrepreneurs within your firm
- Techniques for hiring entrepreneurial people
- Techniques for encouraging entrepreneurial behavior

Building Entrepreneurial People
Examination for Self-Study CPE Credit

Chapter 1: Introduction

True or False?

1. Although many rainmakers are born that way, these skills can be learned.
2. The market for accounting services is not shrinking; fewer companies are doing the kinds of services themselves that CPA firms once provided exclusively.
3. A significant number of small local practices have been created as spin-offs of numerous larger CPA firms and the shrunken Big Eight.
4. More individuals than ever before are interested in working for national CPA firms.
5. Trickle-down theory has taken hold; many companies believe they are being better served by local practices than by national firms.
6. The cost of doing business for CPAs in the 1990s has increased dramatically over that in the 1980s—while partners' salaries have been relatively flat.
7. Clients have become more fee-sensitive, and loyalty has virtually disappeared.

Chapter 2: CPAs Are Reluctant Entrepreneurs

True or False?

1. CPAs learn in college that the key to success in the accounting profession is building one's practice, rather than mere technical expertise.
2. The accounting profession generally attracts a well-rounded type of person, one with a great deal of personality and acumen for building a practice.
3. CPAs think they have no time to sell and use time constraints as a handy excuse.
4. Personal marketing skills still are not required for partnership or advancement in many CPA firms.
5. Taking risks is generally encouraged in the CPA firm environment.
6. The vast majority of CPAs know how to sell themselves effectively.
7. CPAs mistakenly presume their clients know what they need and will ask for it when they want it.
8. CPAs are helped in the business development effort if they have a set plan of action to accomplish business development results.
9. If the CPA firm's leaders do not actively participate in the practice building process, their staff won't either.

Chapter 3: Obstacles to Effective Business Development

True or False?

1. Regarding practice development, most accounting firms willingly invest in marketing and practice development efforts.
2. Accountants, as a rule, are quite confident in their superior selling skills and appreciate the value of selling new business.
3. Most firms use a compensation system that motivates people to actively bring in business.
4. Some partners take credit for business brought in by others, thus damaging the business development effort.

5. Accountants tend to look for a quick fix regarding business development concerns and problems.

6. Most CPA firms simply do not have an entrepreneur-friendly environment.

7. Most accounting firms are headed by dynamic business-development oriented leaders who encourage new business development.

Chapter 4: Producing Entrepreneurs

True or False?

1. Bringing entrepreneurial people into the accounting firm environment will not have an effect on the business development effort.

2. Most firms already have formalized internal mentoring programs to teach people successful business development methods.

3. There are four distinct ways to build rainmakers within your firm: You can acquire them, you can mentor them, you can hire them, and you can encourage the ones you already have.

4. There are three distinct types of mentoring programs your firm can initiate to encourage entrepreneurial behavior and promote active personal marketing: Partner-to-partner mentoring, partner-to-staff mentoring, and staff-to-staff mentoring.

5. It's wise to have partners hold each other accountable for business development efforts and results as part of a mentoring program.

6. Partners should meet with their staff on a regular basis to discuss the staff's business development efforts.

7. It's not important that mentoring programs be conducted on a consistent basis.

Chapter 5: Hiring Entrepreneurs

True or False?

1. Recruiting and hiring have no effect on the business development process in the CPA firm.

2. It becomes much more difficult to let employees go after you have invested training and education in them.

3. It is advisable to be direct with prospective employees about what will expected from them as an employee of the firm and what it will take to get ahead.

4. Marketing problems can be avoided if the right people are hired initially.

5. CPAs already possess certain winning traits that only the best salespeople have.

6. It's not important to hire people who are immediately likable as they can develop their personalities after they become partners.

7. It's a good idea to concentrate on prospective employees' outside activities and social interests to see if they have future business-building potential.

8. It's a good idea to have your best business producers do the initial and final interviewing.

Chapter 6: Developing Entrepreneurs—Emulating the Right Role Models

True or False?

1. Creating an entrepreneurial culture in your firm starts with the hiring process.

2. It's best not to tell future employees what will be expected of them, because you don't want to scare them away.

3. People are easy to change. If your employees or future hires don't possess certain traits, they will gladly change in order to get ahead.

4. Technicians tend to hire other technicians.

Chapter 7: Developing Entrepreneurs—Guiding Rainmakers

True or False?

1. You need not worry about client relationships because clients rarely change accounting firms.

2. Staff members have almost no effect on the client relationship.

3. It is not advisable to allow staff members to talk to and build relationships with their client counterparts.

4. It's best to shelter your employees from the higher-ups at your clients' businesses.

5. There's no need to worry about promoting nonproducers to the partnership.

6. Staff members should not be expected to read industry journals on their own time to supplant their knowledge of the clients' businesses.

7. It's a good idea to suggest that staff members develop a working relationship with their own mentors, within or outside the firm

Chapter 8: Developing Entrepreneurs—Encouraging Entrepreneurial Behavior

True or False?

1. It's a good idea to ask your staff members to withhold their involvement in organizations until they are expert accountants, perhaps five years after you've hired them.

2. It's a good idea to encourage your employees to stay in contact with people they went to school with and turn classmates into future referral sources.

3. All of your professionals should take visible leadership roles inside and outside the firm.

4. It's best to hoard all the administrative duties within the partnership.

5. CPAs should never become friends with their referral sources, as it infringes on the independence and arm's-length nature of the profession.

6. All outside community involvements and activities should be on employees' own time, and they should pay for it themselves, even if it means giving up vacation days and out-of-pocket expenses.

7. It's a good idea to encourage staff members to look for new ways to help clients.

8. It's wise to have your staff members develop an area of expertise.

Chapter 9: Developing Entrepreneurs—
Accountability, Support, and Management

True or False?

1. Because CPAs are professionals, it's not necessary to hold them accountable for practice development.

2. Monetary incentives should be paid for the life of the client. This provides an ongoing motivator to the person continuing to receive bonus checks.

3. Many firms miss a tremendous opportunity by not compensating for new work sold to existing clients.

4. You must help your people experience as many sales and personal marketing successes as possible in order to make them entrepreneurial.

5. Compensation for marketing, selling, and organizational activities must be part of everyone's annual review for a salary increase.

6. It's a good idea to encourage and allow for failure in personal marketing and selling.

7. It's a good idea to invest the majority of your time, effort, energy, and resources in those who are most reluctant and have the smallest possibility of becoming business developers.

8. Nobody should be expected to do personal marketing and selling during the busiest times of the year.

9. Partners should not need to be monetarily motivated for bringing in business.

10. Partners do not need to set an example for everyone else in the firm regarding personal marketing and selling, as they have already paid their dues.

11. A consistent, monitored business development effort is more effective than one that runs in spurts.

12. You must keep the business development process focused on purposeful activity, not only on results.

13. Most CPA firms don't want to have sales meetings because it takes up time that could be billed to their clients.

Chapter 10: Motivating People to Action

True or False?

1. CPA firms have little or no problem keeping their budding superstars.

2. The most obvious way to improve morale and motivate people is to put yourself in their shoes and treat them as they would want to be treated.

3. It's not important to allow your employees to help create the firm-wide goals for new business brought in.

4. What is going on with the firm is of no concern to the staff person.

5. Fear is the best motivator.

6. You should never compensate for unsolicited compliments about employees from clients.

7. It's a good idea to allow your employees to help you run the business.

8. Expanding your practice creates a space for your best employees.

9. Everyone should have his or her own personal marketing plan.

10. In changing your firm, you will face an uphill battle.

Building Entrepreneurial People Self-Study CPE Program

CPE Program Price: $39 • Area of Study: Management • **Recommended Credit Hours: 4**

Please record your CPE answers in the space provided on the left and return this page for scoring. Simply place the completed answer sheet in a stamped envelope and mail it to:

Executive Reports CPE Coordinator,
Harcourt Brace Professional Publishing
525 B Street, Suite 1900
San Diego, California, 92101-4495

METHOD OF PAYMENT

☐ **Payment enclosed ($39.00).**

(Make checks payable to Harcourt Brace & Company.)

Please add appropriate sales tax.
Be sure to sign your order below.

Charge my:
☐ MasterCard   ☐ Visa   ☐ American Express

Account number _____

Expiration date _____
Please sign below for all credit card orders.

☐ **Bill me.** *Be sure to sign your order below.*

NAME _____

FIRM NAME _____

ADDRESS _____

PHONE (___) _____

CPA LICENSE # _____

ISBN: 0-15-601712-1

TO ORDER: Call Toll-Free 1-800-831-7799   Signature _____

See the reverse side of this page for the CPE evaluation.

Building Entrepreneurial People
CPE Answers

Chapter 1
1. _____
2. _____
3. _____
4. _____
5. _____
6. _____
7. _____
8. _____

Chapter 2
1. _____
2. _____
3. _____
4. _____
5. _____
6. _____
7. _____
8. _____

Chapter 3
1. _____
2. _____
3. _____
4. _____
5. _____
6. _____
7. _____

Chapter 4
1. _____
2. _____
3. _____

Chapter 5
1. _____
2. _____
3. _____

Chapter 6
1. _____
2. _____
3. _____

Chapter 7
1. _____
2. _____
3. _____
4. _____
5. _____
6. _____
7. _____

Chapter 8
1. _____
2. _____
3. _____

Chapter 9
1. _____
2. _____
3. _____
4. _____
5. _____
6. _____
7. _____
8. _____
9. _____
10. _____
11. _____
12. _____
13. _____

Chapter 10
1. _____
2. _____
3. _____
4. _____
5. _____
6. _____
7. _____
8. _____
9. _____
10. _____

Building Entrepreneurial People CPE Evaluation

1. Were you informed in advance of the:
   a. Objectives of the course? Y N
   b. Experience level needed to complete the course? Y N
   c. Program content? Y N
   d. Nature and extent of preparation necessary? Y N
   e. Teaching method? Y N
   f. Number of CPE credit hours? Y N

2. Do you agree with the publisher's assessment of:
   a. Objectives of the course? Y N
   b. Experience level needed to complete the course? Y N

   c. Program content? Y N
   d. Nature and extent of advance preparation necessary? Y N
   e. Teaching method? Y N
   f. Number of CPE credit hours? Y N

3. Was the material relevant? Y N

4. Was the presentation of the material effective? Y N

5. Did the program increase your professional competence? Y N

6. Was the program content timely and effective? Y N

Please make any other comments that you feel would improve this course. We appreciate the time you take to complete this questionnaire. Be assured that all of your comments will be considered carefully.

_____

_____

_____

_____

_____

Index

Accountability for business development, 8, 9, 17, 82–83
Accountants. *See* CPA firms; CPA firm staff
Action plans, 8, 9, 12, 81, 85–88
Articles, 68
Attorneys, compared with accountants, 50

Billable hours, 4–5, 58, 67
Bonuses. *See* Compensation systems
Brainstorming, 17
Business cards, 79
Business development
    concentrating upon, 34–35
    control functions and responsibility for, 14, 61–62, 71–74, 81, 82–83
    importance of, 1–2
    obstacles to, 11–14
    offering new or specialized services, 7–8, 39, 59–60, 61, 74
    skills necessary for, 20–26
    see also Developing entrepreneurs; Entrepreneurs; Motivating entrepreneurs

Candidates for employment, traits to look for, 26–28
Change, importance of, 75, 84
Clients
    building referrals and relationships, 41–44, 46–48, 52
    entertaining, 40, 58–59
    importance of finding, 1
    offering new services to, 7–8, 59, 74
    offering specialized services to, 39, 59–60, 61, 74
    pursuing, 35–36, 39–40, 44–45
    retaining, 10, 33–34
    surveys of, 25, 50
Common sense as uncommon, 25, 38
Communication skills, 20, 22
Community service, 55–56
Compensation systems
    limitations of, 9
    monetary incentives for business development, 63–65, 69–70, 76, 77–78, 81, 83, 86
    promotion as incentive to business development, 49–52, 59, 63, 69, 81
Computer services, 8, 82

Consulting arrangements
    nonattest, 2
    outside help for business development planning, 12
CPA firms
    acquisitions and mergers of, 1, 3
    acquisitions of entrepreneurial, 15
    challenges of future for, 2, 3
    importance of business development, 1–2
    improving office environment, 82
    offering new services, 7–8, 59, 74
    reasons for lack of entrepreneurship, 5–6, 8–10, 13
    specializing for client services, 39, 59–60, 61, 74
CPA firm staff
    as "business doctors," 49
    empowering, 57, 79
    expanding contacts with clients, 46, 48, 52, 65, 83
    importance of business development, 11, 59
    improving relationships and morale, 42, 75, 83
    as potentially entrepreneurial, 20–21
    prospective employees, 20, 26–28, 29–31
    specialization in service niches, 39, 59–60, 61, 74
    surveys of, 75–76, 78
    technicians versus rainmakers, 4, 6, 7, 36, 50–51
    as typically nonentrepreneurial, 1, 2, 4–5, 7–8, 10, 13
Creativity, 24, 31

Decision-making skills, 25, 30
Developing entrepreneurs
    action plan steps, 85–88
    career perspective as "business doctors," 48–49
    community service, 55–56
    creating/mentoring, 15–16, 53, 68
    encouraging client relationships, 46–47, 52, 58
    goal setting, 9, 17, 65–67, 76
    importance of leadership and example, 10, 12–13, 14, 25, 67, 70
    leadership and communications skills, 52, 55–56

Developing entrepreneurs, *cont.*
networking, 54–55, 57–58
providing training, 12, 13, 62–63, 83–84
recognition and rewards for, 9, 12, 18, 25, 42, 65–66, 67, 68, 82
responsibility and authority, 57, 61–62
sales management programs, 62, 71–74, 81, 82–83
specializing for client services, 39, 59–60, 61, 74
tying promotion to business development, 49–52, 59, 63, 69, 81
training, 12, 13, 62–63
see also Motivating entrepreneurs
Documenting sales opportunities, 21
Dugan, Mike, 43

Employees (of CPA firms). *See* CPA firm staff
Empowering staff, 57, 79
Emulating entrepreneurial behavior. *See* under entrepreneurs
Entrepreneurs
acquiring through mergers or acquisitions of successful firms, 15
affinity for consultant roles, 2
emulating, 85
building client-referrals and relationships, 41–44
concentrating on business development, 34–35
pursuing opportunities, 35–36
selecting market targets, 39–40
sensible cost-cutting, 36–38
working smarter, 32–34
freeing from detail work, 47–48, 70
hiring, 19–20, 85
importance of action plans, 8
see also Developing entrepreneurs; Motivating entrepreneurs
Entrepreneurship
reasons for lack of, 4–10
value of outside direction, 12
see also Business development
Expense of business development
budgeting for, 62–65, 79
entertaining existing clients, 5, 40, 58–59
importance of continuing in recessionary times, 36–38
as investment versus cost, 11, 25

Failure as okay, 65–66, 74, 78–79
rejection survival, 23, 30
Fensin, Dan, 16, 27, 58, 64
Flexibility, 25–26, 31

Gates, Bill, 6
Getty, J. Paul, 27, 70
Goal setting, 9, 17, 65–67, 76
accountability for business development, 8, 9, 17, 82–83
Greenwald, Gerald, 43

Iacocca, Lee, 6
Interviewing
CPA familiarity with skills for, 20
questions to ask, 29–31
settings for, 28
who should conduct, 28–29

Johnson, John, 42

Koltin, Allan, 59–60

Leadership
importance in entrepreneurs, 52
importance in partners, 10, 12–13, 14, 25, 67, 70
importance in prospective employees, 27

Marketing. *See* Business development
Meetings
expanding contacts of staff with clients, 46, 48, 52, 65, 83
lunchtime salesmanship, 5, 58
mixers with other professional firms, 57–58
partner-to-partner, 16–17
partner-to-staff, 17–18
for sales management, 71–74
Mentoring programs, 15–18, 53, 68
Mergers, 1, 3
Messing, Steven, 19, 27–28, 33, 58
Monetary rewards. *See* Compensation systems; Recognition and rewards for entrepreneurial efforts
Motivating entrepreneurs
action plan steps, 87–88
communicating, 76–77, 78
compensating for personal marketing, 76, 77–78, 81, 83
empowering staff, 57, 79
expense allowances, 79
failure as okay, 78–79

goal setting, 76
keeping stars, 80–81
knowing and empathizing with staff, 75, 83
making room for more partners, 79–80
praising, 81–82
recognition and rewards for entrepreneurial efforts, 9, 12, 18, 25, 42, 65–66, 67, 68, 82
training, 83–84
see also Developing entrepreneurs
Motivation
ability to instill in others, 25
desire to make a difference, 24
seeking in potential new hires, 26, 29
see also Recognition and rewards for entrepreneurial efforts

Networking, 54–55, 57–58
Nisberg, Jay, 2
Nonattest consulting, 2, 3, 64

Organizational skills, 21
Outside activities, 55–56
pursuit on employees' own time, 56

Partners and partnerships
committing to keep staff superstars, 80
entrepreneurs as, 5, 15, 49–52
importance of leadership and example from, 10, 12–13, 14, 25, 67, 70
importance of respect for, 83
mentoring programs, 16–18, 53, 68
tying to business development, 49–52, 59, 63, 69, 81
Peer pressure, 74
Persuasion skills, 25, 31
Planning for business development, 8, 9, 12, 81, 85–88
Promotion to partner, tying to business

development, 49–52, 59, 63, 69, 81
Prospective employees
traits to look for, 26–28
see also Interviewing
Pruitt, Bill, 62
Publishing articles, 68

Rainmakers. *See* Entrepreneurs
Recognition and rewards for entrepreneurial efforts, 9, 12, 18, 25, 42, 65–66, 67, 68, 82
monetary incentives, 63–65, 69–70, 76, 77–78, 81, 83, 86
Referrals, 25, 36, 40, 41, 43–44
Rejection survival, 23, 30
failure as okay, 65–66, 74, 78–79
Relationship skills
with clients, 41–43, 46, 58
importance of, 22, 23, 31
staff responsibilities for, 46–48, 52
toward staff, 42, 75, 83
Reporting systems for sales efforts, 71, 72
Retirements, 3, 47, 80
Risk-taking, 5–6, 22–23, 65–66

Salaries. *See* Compensation systems
Salesmanship. *See* Business development; Developing entrepreneurs
Sales management, 62, 71–74, 81, 82–83.*See also* Business development
Specializing for client services, 39, 59–60, 61, 74
Staffs (of CPA firms). *See* CPA firm staff
Surveys
of clients, 25, 50
of staff, 75–76, 78

Time management, 4–5, 24, 36, 58–59, 69
staff efforts on own time, 52, 56
Training, 83–84
budgeting for, 62–63
obstacles to, 13, 62
value of outside direction, 12